Mascot Mania

Edited by

Sabrina Barlow, Betty Burdett,
Damien Carey, Urania Fung,
Patricia Healy, Tamara Hill,
Amanda Huffer, Kelly Rowan,
Christina Tonan, Gary Wilkens

Texas Review
Huntsville, Texas

Mascot Mania

FIRST EDITION, 2005

Cover design by Amanda Huffer and Kelley Rowan

Library of Congress Cataloging-in-Publication Data

Mascot mania : spirit of Texas high schools / edited by Sabrina Barlow ... [et al.].-- 1st ed.
p. cm.
Includes bibliographical references and index.
ISBN 1-881515-72-9 (alk. paper)
1. School mascots--Texas. 2. High schools--Texas. I. Barlow, Sabrina.
LB3633+

2004028531

Dedicated to all mascots, dead and alive, from
high schools all over the great state of Texas

Table of Contents

Foreword

Mascot Mania is the result of many hours of research and writing and editing by my graduate English 531 class (Practicum: Editing and Publishing) during the fall semester of 2004.

It seemed to us that a state as large and diverse as Texas and with as many high schools as it has deserved a book devoted to cataloging schools and their mascots and in many instances discussing the backgrounds of some of our more unusual mascots. So we set about doing all the research that you find presented in this unique volume.

This book was researched, written, and edited almost exclusively by the students of that class. If there are inaccuracies, so be it: With so many schools and mascots, there will be occasional omissions and errors. And oftentimes the editors were stuck with poor-quality images that they downloaded from web sites. If there are typos, the students must take the blame: This was their baby all the way, warts and all.

Our gratitude to all the high schools who provided graphics and information for this book, and my thanks for the tireless work of the students in that class, whose names are listed as editors on the cover and title page, and to Dan Sellers, for his long hours of intern supervision.

Paul Ruffin, Director
Texas Review Press

Introduction

The Mighty, Mighty Mascot

Mankind has always admired the power and beauty of the creatures who share his world, and has sought to entrap, embody and employ the energy of not only animals but even forces of nature, mythological figures, and human heroes for his tribes, nations, militaries, religions, and sports teams. We here in Texas are no different, and have carried this fascination to new levels in the form of the beloved mascots who cheer on our local high school sports teams.

If mascots began as symbols of power and pride, nothing represents the power and pride of the typical Texas town like its high school football team. We all know that Friday night is football night, and at the sidelines of every game, whether it be a cross-town rivalry or the state championship, the school's mascot is sure to be found: clowning, cheering, pranking, prancing, being beat up, and above all rallying the team to victory. Mascots generate and focus that all-important force known as school spirit, which often seems to make all the difference on the field, not to mention in the heart of every student, fan, and alum. Then there's the other side's mascot, who is likely beat out only by the ref as the least popular figure in the stadium. Mascots are crucial to the high school football experience, and it would be hard to imagine a game without them to cheer or jeer. Every school depends on its mascot to enliven the team and bring that sweet gridiron glory to town.

Mascots being so central to a community's sense of style and self, it seems only natural to ask how these names and symbols came about and what they mean. This book was created to answer this question and highlight the many thrilling, wacky, or outright weird mascots cheered on by fans across the state of Texas. Mascots derive their names and faces from several sources: the town's name or history, local geography or economy, or a fortunate alliteration that sounds tough and proud. A few were chosen just because they were odd enough to stand out. Mascots are about fun, pride, competitive spirit, and community identity. One thing is always true about a Texas high school mascot: the school loves its mascot and the mascot loves the team. Why else would a man dance around under hot lights in a heavy tiger suit?

Mascot Mania explores the many intriguing facets of the Texas high school mascot and the unique culture which surrounds it. We intend this book to serve as a fun and factual guide to the wide world of the Texas high school mascot, and be a unique source of pleasure and pride for all those who have ever cheered on those Texas Eagles, Wildcats, Longhorns, Bulldogs, Mustangs and Hornets. Or even the Hippos, Gorillas, and Mighty Mites!

Gary Wilkins

Disclaimer

"Finish each day and be done with it. You have done what you could; some blunders and absur-ditites have crept in; forget them as soon as you can. Tomorrow is a new day; you shall begin it serenely and with too high a spirit to be encum-bered with your old nonsense."

- Ralph Waldo Emerson

Chapter 1

The History of the Mascot

"History, although sometimes made up of the few acts of the great, is more often shaped by the many acts of the small."

—Mark Twain

History of the Mascot

What is the origin and meaning of the word mascot? What do different mascots signify? Why is it that school mascots are mainly an American phenomenon, and who adopted the first mascot? Hopefully after reading this book, you will be able to connect ancient traditions to modern practices.

The earliest evidence of mascots dates back to the cave paintings thousands of years ago, but the word *mascot* only entered the English language in 1881, borrowed from the French *mascotte*, meaning *charm*. The French adopted the word from the Provencal *mascoto*, meaning *sorcery fetish*, which evolved from *masco*, meaning *witch*. *Masco* came from the Medieval Latin *masca*, meaning *mask*, *specter*, and *witch*. The word was popularized by *La Mascotte*, a French opera about a farm girl who brought good luck to whoever possessed her. The opera ran for over one thousand performances and became so popular that it was translated into English in 1881. The translated title became *The Mascot*. By 1882, the opera made its way to the United States, and the concept of the mascot as a person, animal, or object bringing good luck has stuck ever since.

Historically, mascots personified animal traits that men admired—the courage of the lion, the strength of the bear. For example, the eagle, who is a representative of many great nations, including the U.S., is one of the most admired birds of prey. The fact that it can soar to great heights and feed from the land, spending little time hunting, reflects much about its hidden significance as a symbol. Every society that had contact with this powerful bird developed a mythology about it. It is interesting to connect the similar mythologies that were formed on different continents so many years ago. For example, compare the Greek god Zeus to the Native American Thunderbird. Zeus would often change into an eagle to control thunder and rain. The thunderbird, most often depicted as an eagle by Native Americans, also controls lightning and rain, punishment and reward. To the Plains Cree, all eagles have mystical powers, and these powers can be shared by anyone who possesses part of the bird. In Egyptian hieroglyphics, the eagle was the symbol for the soul, spirit, and warmth of life. This bird was a strong emblem for the Roman Empire as well, associated with the Roman god Jupiter. The Hittites used a double-headed eagle as an emblem so as never to be surprised. Even the early Christians saw the eagle as a symbol of resurrection.

Spirit building has become a peculiarly American phenomenon. In fact, most schools around the globe have not adopted the use of mascots. It is believed that the modern American mascot is a byproduct of traditions that have been native to the Americas for thousands of years. There is much in common between a tribal elder doing a fertility dance in a mask and animal skin and a giant grinning gorilla leading a cheer at the homecoming game: Both, in a sense, use the mascot to bring good fortune. In addition, the Native Americans use the mascot for good fortune in harvest, for protection against misfortune, to heal the sick, and to cause misfortune among their enemies.

Traditionally, the mascot is usually adopted upon the opening of a high school. But this convention hasn't always been so. Central High School of Philadelphia, Pennsylvania, opened in 1838, and Lockport Union School opened in 1848; neither school had a mascot upon opening. Back in 1897, football teams referred to themselves solely by school names—for example, Brockton High vs. Bridgewater Normal School. In fact, the trend of adopting high school mascots was not popularized until the 1920s.

It all started with baseball. Although the first professional teams were formed in 1845, they were usually referred to by their team name or home city. Because baseball was considered the "knickerbocker sport," the fans started identifying teams by the color of their socks: hence the names the New York Knickerbockers, now the Yankees, and the Cincinnati Red Stockings, which evolved into the Red Legs, then finally into the Reds. Although the Boston Red Sox team was founded in 1893, it wasn't until 1907 that it adopted the Red Sox as its nickname. Prior to that, it was referred to as the Bostons or the Boston Baseball Club. The Cleveland Indians went through several nicknames. Prior to 1887, it was known as The Forest City's Team. In 1888, the owner renamed the team the Cleveland Spiders because the players were skinny and poor fielders. The Spiders hired one of the first Native Americans in the majors—Louis Francis Sockalexis. The term Indians was reportedly given to the team by disrespectful fans around the country. Sockalexis was not well received by the baseball fans, and in less than three years and only 367 at-bats, Sockalexis was out of baseball for good. In 1915, two years after his death, the nickname Spiders was officially changed to the Indians.

Meanwhile, in 1867, football was introduced for the very first time, and colleges began organizing football games. Princeton and Rutgers College led the way in establishing some rudimentary rules. On November 6, 1869, Rutgers and Princeton played their very first intercollegiate football game. Rutgers won by a score of six goals to four. At that time, Rutgers was officially known as the Queen's College, and the athletic teams were referred to as the Queen's Men, but it wasn't until 1925 that a true mascot was chosen. Due to its chicken-like attributes, that mascot didn't stick. Rutgers is now known as the Scarlet Knights.

Princeton didn't officially adopt a mascot until 1923, but in the early 1880s the football players proudly sported their orange and black school colors. They wore broad orange and black stripes on their stockings and jerseys, and sometimes on stocking caps. Watching their movements in the waning light of late autumn afternoons, sportswriters began to call them tigers. By 1889, "the tiger" appeared in a Princeton song by Clarence Mitchell beginning with "The Orange and the Black." In 1923, a live tiger that had been captured in India by the father of football player Albert F. Howard was brought to Princeton as a mascot.

But it is Yale who claims to be the first university in the United States to have adopted a mascot—"Handsome Dan." In 1889 Andrew B. Graves purchased a dog from a New Haven blacksmith for $5.00. The students dubbed him the "Yale mascot." He was always led across the field just before football and baseball games began. He was said to look like a cross between an alligator and a horned frog, and he was called "handsome" under the law of compensation. He was always taken to games on a leash, and the Harvard football team for years owed its continued existence to the fact that the rope held. *The Philadelphia Press* recalled that "a favorite trick was to tell him to 'Speak to Harvard.' He would bark ferociously and work himself into physical contortions of rage never before dreamed of by a dog." According to fans, Dan was peculiar in one thing—he would never associate with anyone but students.

Along with the widespread growth of football among the states' high schools through the 1890s and early 1900s came the development of the traditional arch rivalries, which have always been one of the keys to the game's great popularity. Usually pitting schools from neighboring communities, these annual games quickly became the focal point of every football season for the two schools involved. The first recorded interscholastic game took place on November 1, 1879, in Illinois. Unfortunately, the first high school to adopt a mascot is unknown.

By the 1920s the concept of mascots started to catch on. So by the time the National Football League organized, Bulldogs, Cardinals, and Tigers were already strutting down the fields, and this is about the time many high schools began adopting mascots. Now we constantly hear contests for sports teams adopting new or changing old mascots. All want to find a mascot who will accurately represent their team's spirit. The mascot is no longer a passive nickname that is given to a team by fans but is now a power symbol that directly represents the attributes the team reflects or wants to possess. Anyone stepping onto a sporting field costumed as a mascot is joining a very long tradition dating back to the start of civilization itself.

Chapter 2

Mascot Stories

"I am forced to conclude that God made Texas on his day off, for pure entertainment, just to prove that all that diversity could be crammed into one section of earth by a really top hand."

—Mary Lasswel

DUDES

"A born Texan has instilled in his system
a mind-set of no retreat or no surrender.
I wish everyone the world over had the
dominating spirit that motivates Texans."
—Billy Clayton

Blue Devils
Central Heights High School

The school was built in 1925 on a site in the center of town, hence the name Central Heights High School. The mascot was chosen to commemorate front-line French fighters of WWI —The Blue Devils—a group similar to U.S. Marines, as only the strongest and most physically able men were chosen to be in these "shock troops."

They were the ground warriors who went in first to clear away the enemy, and they were always as chivalrous off the battlefield as they were heroic upon it. Central Heights chose them for their valor and heroism because they were respected even by the enemy.

Chieftains and Squaws
Friona High School

History teaches that Native Americans were the first inhabitants of what is now known as the United States of America. It is recorded that Native American tribes were led by one chief who had several followers to help him colonize an area. This colonizing spirit of the Indian Chief was captured in Friona in 1908 when Miss Roxie Witherspoon started the first Friona School in a one-room building with fifteen to eighteen students.

The school continued to grow and a new, two-story, red brick building was constructed from 1911-1912. Less than ten years later, a lightning storm destroyed the new building and the school was temporarily relocated to a local church. While they were still housed in the church, Friona High School basketball player Bill Buyer suggested that the team choose the Chieftains to be the school mascot. Chieftains was a fitting name because the residents literally weathered the storm and proved that they shared the tenacity of their Native American forefathers by refusing to let a setback deter them from their goal of providing students with an education.

Friona High School was eventually rebuilt in 1924 and the Chieftains were adopted into Texas mascot history. According to Buyer, the red color represents the "red blooded, fighting original Americans," and the white color represents the integrity that is associated with athletic activities.

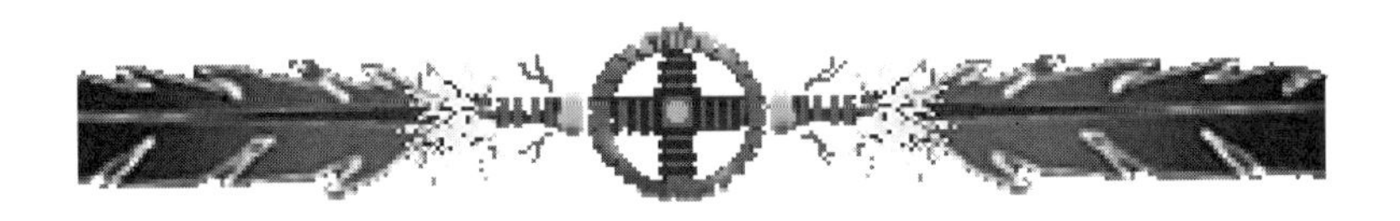

Exporters
Brazosport High School

Back in the early 1950s when the school was in its infancy, Brazosport High School had a big cannon that they shot off at the football games. The UIL folks didn't care for that too much, so the school was forced to give up that cannon. The "doers" of the community met regularly at Rasberry's Restaurant for coffee and discussions and took it upon themselves to come up with a mascot for the Brazosport team. Because Freeport is a port city on the Brazos River, the team had been unofficially called the Ships or Shippers. This group of freethinkers decided to build a wooden ship that they put on wheels and pulled around the field when the team made a touchdown, which became their "mascot." The name Exporters came out of one of their sessions at the restaurant and it stuck. In the mid-80s, the school added a mascot in the form of a student dressed like a sailor, wearing a gigantic head, who ran around with the ship and helped lead the cheers. The school symbol is an anchor. The girls' athletic teams are called the Ladyships. The dance/drill team is called the Shipmates.

Indians
Quanah High School

Quanah High School, as well as the town where it's located, is named after the famous Native American Quanah Parker. The Quanah High School mascot is the Indian. Quanah Parker was the last Chief of the Comanches. His was the last tribe in the Staked Plains to come under the reservation system.

Fighting Irish
Cathedral High School

The impact of St. Patrick, the patron saint of Ireland, stretched beyond holidays and religion when he became a factor in the choosing of a mascot for Cathedral High School of El Paso, Texas, a Roman Catholic high school for young men. The school is administered by the De La Salle Christian Brothers, a religious order of teachers founded in France in 1679 by St. John Baptist de La Salle.

The elementary school near Cathedral High School is called St. Patrick's Cathedral. By association, Cathedral High School chose the Fighting Irish as their mascot.

Marauders
Marcus High School

Marcus High School in Lewisville originally opened as a ninth-grade school. Committees of administrators and teachers from four different areas—The Colony, Lewisville, Highland Village, and Flower Mound—were formed to seek input from students. Middle-school students also had some input. Their three finalists for mascot were the Panthers, Raiders, and Marauders. The vote was so close that there had to be a runoff vote between Raiders and Marauders. Marauders won along with the school colors—red and silver. A funny twist is that all the ninth graders and middle-school students who voted actually ended up graduating from Lewisville High School. Marcus remained a ninth-grade school for several more years. There are no other Marauders mascots in the state of Texas.

Pirates
Pine Tree High School

Pine Tree High School got its name from the tree under which school was held in the 1840s. The Pine Tree High School's mascot, the Pirate, was chosen by its first football coach, Richard A. Crawford, in 1934. Coach Crawford was a fan of the Pittsburgh Pirates. He thought *Pirates* sounded good with *Pine Tree*, and the Pine Tree High School mascot was born.

A former school teacher, Annie Lou Mitcham Utzman, helped raise money for team uniforms through donations and a benefit dance at the Blue Bird Dance Hall. According to her daughter, Lou Gene Henderson, Ms. Utzman chose the school colors, blue and gold.

However, the money covered only eleven uniforms. Every time Coach Crawford sent in an un-uniformed player, a switch of clothing had to occur. A team huddle was used to provide privacy during the change. Players on the small team had to play both offense and defense. Despite their challenges, the Pine Tree High School Pirates won the 1938 district championship. By then the team had enough uniforms, but they weren't all alike.

Punchers
Mason High School

Though the Mason High School athletes started out in the early 1900s known as merely "the football team," they eventually came to identify themselves as the Punchers. The first appearance of this mascot occurred when the yearbook staff referred to the football team as *cowpunchers* in the 1924 Mason High School annual. When the local newspaper picked up the trend in 1927, the name stuck. The name "cowpunchers" was abbreviated to just "punchers" in 1932, initially by the *Mason County News*. Since then, they have created an official mascot named Puncher Pete, who celebrated his 32nd birthday in October of 2004.

The name Punchers is no doubt unique, which may explain the interest that has been shown in its origins for the past forty or so years. One can only imagine the number of times the school has had to field questions from those who have driven by the school's football stadium, The Puncher Dome, and wondered if it really served as a football stadium or a boxing arena. Their curiosity wasn't too far into left field, though, because the stadium hasn't only served the purpose of hosting football games. While never an arena for boxing matches, as would be fitting for the nickname Punchers, it did serve as a horse-racing track when originally built in the 1930s, and then later as a rodeo facility. Today, The Puncher Dome caters only to the events of the Mason High School Athletics Department, and, of course, the Mason Puncher Band.

Even the youngest of the Mason community can tell you what it means to be a Puncher. He may not give you the definition of a cowpoke, cattle rustler, or buckaroo, but he will tell you that to be a Puncher is to be a Mason Puncher and to be proud of it.

Rebels
Midland Lee High School

The Rebels rode to victory at Midland Lee High School in the 1970s. Midland Lee students celebrated the Rebels by singing their school battle cry: "Whenever any Rebel does well or needs encouragement, I'll fly the *Battle Flag* with PRIDE." The Rebels were closely associated with American history and were initially represented by the Confederate flag.

In the mid-1990s, the Rebels underwent a makeover—the community decided to remove the Confederate flag from the hands of the official mascot because several students and local residents were offended by the symbolism behind it, especially the flag's connotations with slavery and prejudice. Today, a friendly, more universal character holding a Lee High School Library book represents the Rebels: Yosemite Sam from the popular *Looney Toons* cartoon series. Although the Rebels have undergone years of controversy, they continue to sound their fearless battle cry to all of their competitors.

Rebels
Tascosa High Shool

Tascosa High School, which opened in 1958, switched their mascot from General Reb to the Rebel Kid by changing directions from south to west. According to the school website, "early school symbols were centered around the Old South, but were eventually replaced by a western image." Not only was the name of the rebel mascot altered, but the Confederate flag was replaced.

Rockcrushers
Knippa High School

Knippa High School's donning the name Rockcrushers was not the first instance of a school altering its mascot name to support the town's economic stronghold. When the Knippa County school was established, its mascot was the more traditional representative of the Texas plains, the longhorn. When Vulcan Industries moved into town in the mid-1940s, however, the school district decided that its schools should support the community's largest employer by retiring the longhorn. With so many parents of Knippa school children working for Vulcan Industries' rock-crushing plant, it only made sense that the students would feel a sense of pride and community if they too were called Rockcrushers. Smart move on the part of the district! At least they didn't play with the name of the rockcrushing plant and have all of their students running around with pointy ears and arched eyebrows, giving the Vulcan *hello*, made famous by the character from *Star Trek*, Mr. Spock!

Roughnecks
Columbia High School

His name is Elmo, and he's plenty scary looking. The Columbia High School mascot is a roughneck, named after the oil-field workers who arrived in the 1920s after the discovery of oil in the area. Carrying an ax, Elmo wears a hardhat, a mean scowl, and the letter *C* on his muscled chest.

Vaqueros
San Diego High School

The population of the San Diego Independent School District is 99% Hispanic. The vaqueros, Mexican cowboys, worked on ranches, of which there are many in this district. Therefore, to embody the spirit of the district, San Diego High School adopted vaqueros as its mascot.

Volunteers
James Bowie High School

Remember the Alamo? James Bowie High School does. Its nickname is the Volunteers, but its mascot is better known as Jim Bowie. Bowie was a volunteer at the Alamo. He is better known for his famous Bowie knife and sometimes as a reckless adventurer.

Jim Bowie is now immortalized as one of the true folk heroes in early Texas. Born in Kentucky in 1796, he moved with his family to Louisiana in 1802. It was there that he first acquired a reputation for his bold and fearless disposition. In 1827, Bowie participated in a bloody brawl near Natchez, Mississippi, where several men were killed and Bowie was wounded. After recovering, he moved to Texas.

Bowie took part in many adventures. He spent considerable time cultivating friendships with Indians in his search for the elusive silver and gold reported to be hidden in the interior of Texas. By some accounts, he is said to have found the fabled San Saba mines, also known as the Bowie mines.

In the Texas Revolution, Bowie was a leading participant at the Battle of Concepión and in the Grass Fight near San Antonio. He was in command of a volunteer force in San Antonio when William Travis arrived with regular army troops. The two men shared authority during much of the siege of the Alamo, but pneumonia disabled Bowie, and he was confined to his cot at the time of his death on March 6, 1836, at the battle of the Alamo.

When asked why James Bowie High calls itself Volunteers instead of Bowies, it is rumored that the superintendent who founded the school attended the University of Tennessee, whose mascot is the Volunteers, which also explains the school colors —orange and white and *blue* . . . .

Westerners
Lubbock High School

Since 1891, there has been a Lubbock High. As students walk down the school halls every day, it is important for them to know the rich history behind the school.

In the early history of Lubbock County, when the town sites of old Lubbock and Monterey were still rivals, there was no established school.

In 1891, the two rival towns merged, and the first Lubbock school became a reality. The school announcement offered, "Schooling for all who could reach it by pony, wagon, buggy or on foot."

In 1922, although the school mascot was a Westerner, the football team was named the Pirates. In order for an out-of-town team to come to Lubbock, the school had to agree to pay for transportation, a private meal, and first-class accommodations.

In 1929, enrollment approached 500 and the overcrowding was so serious that the high school was threatened with the loss of accreditation.

In the fall, plans began for the construction of a new high school, which took three years to complete. During that time, it was necessary for many of the grades to go to half-day scheduling. The new school opened on April 1, 1931.

A cowboy, the symbol of the Westerner, now rides a horse at the school's main entrance.

Yoemen
C.H. Yoe High School

The mascot for the C.H. Yoe High School in Cameron, Texas, is the Yoemen. What is the reasoning for adopting a Robin Hood-type mascot with a name that is reminiscent of Geoffrey Chaucer's forester character from *The Canterbury Tales*? This British forester character was suggested by Mrs. C.H. Yoe, the woman who, along with her husband, donated property to the community for the purpose of establishing a home for the high school. Yes, it was a situation of property transferring from the wealthy to the less advantaged. And, yes, it is also coincidental that the benefactors' names are Yoe. But, are these the values inherent in the forester figure that made him stand the test of time with the school?

This is not the first incident of a school taking on a character as a mascot, but the Cameron Yoemen were at least original in changing the spelling of the character's title to reflect the last name of their philanthropists, Mr. and Mrs. Yoe.

This archer dressed in maroon and grey appeared for the first time in the high school newspaper in 1950 and is still a part of the school today. Perhaps it is the history of the archer that endears him to the student body. Perhaps not. Whatever it is, the students are still proud of their representative today.

CRITTERS

"The only things in the middle of the road are yellow stripes and dead armadillos."

—Jim Hightower

Angoras
Rocksprings High School

In a time when Dallas County was transitioning from agricultural pursuits to urban and industrial occupations, the high school in neighboring Edwards County, Rocksprings, was also transitioning. Oddly, their high school made a contradictory transition by changing its more domesticated mascot, the bulldog, to one that more clearly represented the ranching industry of the district. The school kept its colors of red and white, but took the Angora goat as its mascot.

In 1940 when the transitions were occurring, the ranchers of Edwards County stood entirely behind the mascot change of Rocksprings High School. In their minds, this new mascot would not only benefit the school but would also advertise the Rocksprings area as being "The Angora Goat Capital of the World." Rocksprings depends on the production of wool and mohair, and Edwards County is, in fact, one of the world's top producers of these products. The town even hosts a "top-of-the-world" festival to celebrate the town's wool and mohair production.

Bobcats
Hallsville High School

Superintendent J. C. Armstrong established the bobcat as the Hallsville High School mascot in 1927 when the basketball team was formed. Hallsville High School has since obtained a collection of mounted bobcats donated from several individual hunters. State Comptroller John Sharp donated the most recent mounted bobcat to the high school.

The class of 2001 paid for a new drawing of the mascot and it is placed in the entrance of Hallsville High School. Another drawing serves as the letterhead for the high school.

Dragons
Carroll High School

There is a lot of green-dragon pride in the town of Southlake. Every school within the Carroll Independent School District has the dragon for its mascot (featured on front cover). The Carroll football team was the 2004 5A National Champions. Their head football coach, Todd Dodge, is known for developing an amazing offensive program. They have a 72,000-square-foot indoor practice field with an 80-yard field turf surface and a weight room.

Katelyn Cash is a junior at Carroll High School, and this is her third year to wear the dragon costume. When she began her mascot duties, she named her dragon character *Daisy*. Katelyn said, "It takes a little while to get used to it, but after you develop the character, it becomes more of a personality . . . now I don't always have to think of what to do because everything just comes natural." The dragon costume has been passed down to the junior varsity campus.

This year the varsity high school campus acquired its own dragon costume. Katelyn organized a "Name the Mascot" contest, charging students a dollar per vote. The winner received fifty dollars. The proceeds went toward the new dragon costume. Katelyn chose the winning name, *Charlie*, in honor of outstanding Carroll High School football coach Charlie Stallcup, who died of melanoma the previous summer.

Carroll High School sophomore Jordan Allison now wears the *Daisy* dragon costume, while Katelyn wears *Charlie*. The girls say that *Daisy* is "very girly," and that *Charlie* is "macho." *Daisy* wears a big bow on her head and blows kisses, while *Charlie* blows smoke.

At Carroll High School, students go through a mascot tryout procedure that includes a three-day clinic. Students must make props, choose music, and choreograph a routine. The tryout consists of an interview and performance of a two-minute skit before three judges.

Eagles
St. Thomas High School

St. Thomas High School was founded by Basilian priests in 1900. Legend has it that a sportswriter was given credit for dubbing St. Thomas teams the *Toms*. Apparently the headline of an article that had St. Thomas in it was cut off, so the name *Toms* was born. In 1929, Father Thomas O'Rourke, C.S.B., Principal of St. Thomas, decided the eagle should be the official emblem of the school. The school newspaper, once called *The Tom Weekly*, became *The Eagle*. However, it wasn't until 1943 that the athletic teams changed their name from the Toms to the Eagles.

Fighting Bucks
Alpine High School

According to the earliest annual (1946) in the Alpine High School Library, the buck was the mascot and purple and gold were the colors. The colors are still purple and gold (old gold) and the school uses the Notre Dame fight song—which came first is debatable! The buck was decided on due to the fact that Alpine is in mule deer country and hunters flock to the area for the hunting season and the wonderful weather in the mountains of West Texas. The mule deer was also chosen because it is big, strong, fast, agile, and intelligent, and typifies the power Alpine tries to embody in its academics and athletics.

Hippos
Hutto High School

The hippo was adopted as the Hutto High mascot because in 1915 a hippopotamus escaped from a circus train traveling through Austin and was eventually found in a creek near Hutto. It seemed logical at the time.

Kangaroos
Weatherford High School

The kangaroo became the official Weatherford High School mascot in 1922, when Carlos Hartnett, a prominent Weatherford citizen and WHS graduate, suggested it. Prior to this, the team had been called the Morgan Raiders after Del Morgan, an outstanding football player.

After Morgan graduated from WHS, he attended Austin College, which had the kangaroo as its mascot. It was then suggested that the Weatherford High School team be named the Kangaroos, continuing to honor Morgan. At the time, no other high school in the state had this name for its mascot, so it was accepted.

Lions
Spring High School

Spring High School's mascot is a lion named Ulysses. A student is selected during cheerleader tryouts to perform as the mascot for the following year. Ulysses attends all football games and many other athletic events, providing school spirit and a roaring good time. He is truly Spring High School's king of the jungle.

Lobos
Chavez High School

Before Chavez High School opened in 2000, its future students from Stevenson Middle School chose the school colors and the lobo for its mascot. Two years later they gave the mascot a name, Louie. Why Louie? Because the band could play the song "Louie Louie" and the students wanted their mascot to have his own song.

Longhorns
J. Frank Dobie High School

Dobie High School was built in 1968 and named after the Texas author and educator J. Frank Dobie. The first principal of Dobie High School, Allen Sory, decided upon the school's colors and mascot. Sory took it upon himself to mold the school's colors and mascot after the University of Texas where Dobie himself once taught. The colors became orange and white, and the mascot, the fabled Texas longhorn. Even the brick on the outside of the Dobie High School building is burnt orange.

Mavericks
Marshall High School

In the 1924 Marshall High School yearbook, the school team was referred to as The Red and White. In the 1926 yearbook, they had become The Mavericks. *The American Heritage Dictionary of the English Language* defines *maverick* as "[an] unbranded or orphaned range calf or colt, traditionally considered the property of the first person who brands it." Richard Fluker, Public Information Officer for Marshall High School, found "a picture of a bull who had treed some beat-up football players labeled with the names of opponents" in the 1926 yearbook, and the bull logo became official for the school.

Mustangs
Valley High School

Five individuals in Harlingen, Texas, got together and decided to open a charter school seven years ago that would concentrate on the at-risk students. During the process of obtaining a license to educate, they wanted to adopt a mascot that would reflect the students they would work with and the nature of the education they would provide. The student population would be those who had difficulty working within the traditional system, just as the wild mustang had difficulty working in the world of man. It didn't take long to vote on the mustang as the mascot that would reflect the spirit of Valley High School students and the faculty's determination to make a difference in their lives.

Mustangs
Coronado High School

Coronado High School, named for the great Spanish adventurer and explorer Francisco Vasquez de Coronado, opened its doors as the third Lubbock high school in 1965. It is home to the Mustangs, the wild and spirited horses of the west. Coronado boasts scarlet and gold as its school colors and the symbols of its many victories.

Mustangs
James E. Taylor High School

Brenda Pope, secretary at James E. Taylor High School, was there when the doors opened in 1979. According to Ms. Pope, the mustang was chosen as the mascot for the school by the superintendent of the Katy Independent School District, Mr. James E. Taylor, the school's namesake. The first athletic booster club presented a fiberglass mustang to the student body, and it is still present today. Mr. Taylor was a colonel in the U.S. Coast Guard and the mustang's name is Colonel.

Panthers
C.E. King High School

C.E. King High School's panther mascot resembled the 1960s Houston area children's show host Kitirik in that a girl with whiskers painted on her face wore a black leotard, black stockings and a black hood, depicting the panther mascot. The mascot's name was Pepper. A *papier mâché* panther covered in fiberglass came to the high school in 1965 and sat in the entryway. Over the years, the panther image was carried to football games.

Years later, a panther mascot suit was purchased through a fundraiser organized by Ava Brown, the cheerleading sponsor. The costume had a big round cartoon head, replacing the old Pepper image.

A group of students and coaches decided they wanted a "fiercer looking" mascot. Debbie Pilcher, Director of Public Relations, ordered a new costume with a more realistic panther head. Some students preferred the old mascot. A compromise was reached by using both mascot images. The realistic panther costume was called Pepper, and the round cartoon-head costume was called Prissy.

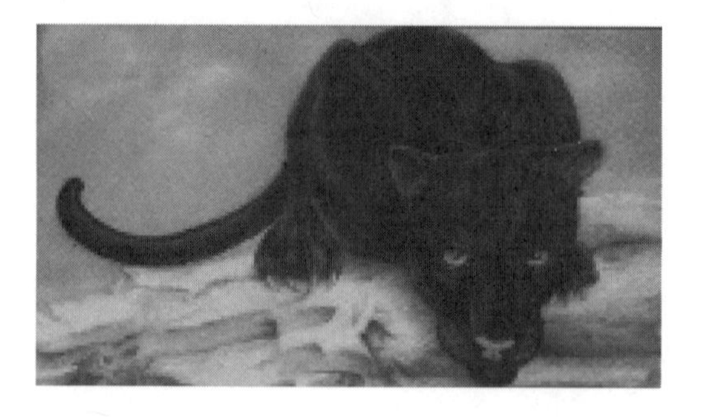

Panthers
Cypress Springs High School

Sarah Harty, principal of Cy-Springs High School relates, "When it was time for Cy-Springs to select a mascot, we polled the middle-school students for suggestions. We assimilated the suggestions and had the students vote. At that point in time, the Jacksonville Jaguars and Carolina Panthers had just formed, so those were the two favorites. The panther itself, though, is named Rudy after our founding head coach, who died the summer before the school opened."

Porcupines
Springtown High School

The unassuming porcupine crawled its way into the history of Springtown High School in the mid-1920s. According to town legend, this spiky creature was elevated to small-town fame when basketball player C.M. "Snake" Hutchinson, nominated the porcupine to be the Springtown High School mascot. Hutchinson believed the porcupine was the ideal candidate for this job: "No one wants to get near a porcupine . . . they don't want . . . to become a target for quills."

Still not convinced that a porcupine is a fierce, scary mascot? In the 1960s, the head cheerleader and several Springtown High School students became believers when the school purchased a live porcupine to serve as its mascot. This small, yet non-cuddly, critter was aptly named Porky. The head cheerleader was responsible for taking care of Porky in between his famous appearances at Springtown High School games and pep rallies. The cheerleader and other students soon discovered there was more "scare" to Porky than his dangerous, prickly quills: He had an odor that would scare opponents out of their seats. "The smell was terrible, quite frankly," said Laurie Moseley III, Director of Instructional Services at Springtown High School. So what is the moral behind this mascot story? Never underestimate the power of a porcupine.

Raccoons
Frisco High School

The Frisco High School Raccoon mascot originated around 1924. As the students and staff discussed what the mascot should be, one of the students suggested that the mascot be named for his pet raccoon, and it stuck. This unique mascot is a part of the recognized tradition and school pride that has been built in this community over the years.

In March of 2002, the FISD Board of Trustees voted that the mascot officially be the full name, *Raccoon*, and not its shortened version. It was felt that this kept the traditions of the community intact, while also being sensitive to any concerns or potential discomfort of current and future students. Their decision was based on one thing—that it was the right thing to do.

Mighty Red Ants
Progreso High School

Progreso is a small town located on the Rio Grande River, one county west of the Gulf of Mexico. Progreso ISD could compete for Texas' smallest district, both in geography and population. However, its diminutive status is not the reason the Progresso High School mascot is the Mighty Red Ant. The story is simple and one of appreciation and loyalty.

There is a middle school named for Dorothy Thompson. She taught generations of Progreso students in the elementary grades when Progreso had only a primary school. She was very popular and much loved. When Ms. Thompson needed to gather her charges together after recess or for assembly, she would call loudly, "Where are my little red ants?" When a high school was finally built in Progresso, it was filled with a population of Ms. Thompson's Little Red Ants. The students decided their mascot should be the same.

"It's not been easy being a Progreso High School Mighty Red Ant," current football coach Elvis Hernandez says. "On the road, the team is often greeted with *Got Raid?* posters and chants of *Stomp the ants*. The Mighty Red Ants are changing their own luck for the better," Hernandez says, "and getting more competitive."

Rhinos
Carnegie Vanguard High School

Carnegie Vanguard High School opened its doors in the year 2002 with 174 students. The students were allowed to vote on any animal they wanted for their mascot. "The school colors are red, white, and blue," said school secretary Beverly Will, "so we expected something patriotic, like an eagle. We were all shocked when they came up with a rhino."

In its third year, Carnegie Vanguard High School has 253 students enrolled. They don't have anyone wearing a rhino costume, but they do have the distinction of being the only school in the state of Texas with a rhino for its mascot.

RoHawks
Randolph High School

In the summer of 1962, Randolph High School was getting ready to open its doors for the first time. A group of students was formed to decide on the school name and mascot. Some wanted to use a name that had something to do with the Air Force Academy, itself still pretty new, or to pick a sort of "junior version" of some already-established school name. One suggestion was the Buttons, but this was immediatley ruled out as too effeminate. The "School Naming Committee," after much heated debate, settled on the hawk as a mascot, since it was a bird of prey and not too far removed from the AFA Falcon. But they weren't finished. In 1962 many people were interested in space exploration, and the rockets were a symbol of that interest. The group began exploring how it could merge the two images, and this resulted in the concept of a hawk on a rocket. However, *Rocket Hawk* just didn't sound right. After much more debate, they settled on *RoHawk*. It was thought to be pretty weird, but that was part of its appeal. The group decided that the really strange name and mascot were so different that people would notice and wouldn't forget. Even though the school has had to endure some public embarrassment because of the general comment—"What the hell is a RoHawk?"—reaction of people when they first hear the name, they have never been forced to change, and Randolph High School is still the home of the RoHawks.

Skeeters
Mesquite High School

Of course, the name of the town *is* Mesquite, so choosing the *Skeeters* as the mascot of the town's high school seems only natural. Those who are accustomed to the Dallas-Fort Worth area of Texas might argue that, regardless of the name of the town, the skeeter mascot would be appropriate for nearly any school in this great state, since mosquitoes seem to outnumber the human population ten to one in the dog days of summer. Either way, Mesquite High School saw the skeeter as a persistent little critter that never strayed from its plan of attack, and that seemed the perfect representative for the high school student body, which strives daily for excellence and achievement.

Thunderbirds
Coronado High School

In the mythology of the Indians of North America, birds play a very prominent role. Of all of them, the thunderbird is the most frequently encountered. Growing out of the effort of primitive man to account for the natural phenomena surrounding him, the myth of the thunderbird varies with almost every tribe, but it is usually held accountable for lightning, thunder, and rain. The symbols vary from tribe to tribe. With some, it is shaped like an eagle, with others like a hawk, with others like a grouse, and others consider it a monster of unknown form. The wide extent of this myth is evidenced by the fact that the thunderbird is pictured dwelling in the mountains with kindred spirits and sallying forth at intervals to cause lightning by enveloping its wings while the rain falls from a lake carried on its back. To the primitive people of the arid Southwest, water is the most precious of all elements. The Southwestern Indian depended chiefly upon his crops, flocks, and herds for livelihood. This was particularly true of the Pueblo. To them, the coming of the thunderbird meant rich grass for their flocks and herds, abundant crops and full granaries, and so the bird was a deity embodying all things beneficial and kind. Its presence is a constant omen of peace and happiness.

Tigers
Spring Woods High School

Spring Woods High School opened in 1964. A school board member was a Louisiana State University alumnus with a fondness for its mascot. Hence, Spring Woods High School's mascot became the tiger. According to Jim McNiel, Technology Specialist at Spring Woods, "The colors black and yellow were the favorite of the then school superintendent, Mr. Landrum."

Unicorns
New Braunfels High School

In 1928, New Braunfels High School adopted the heraldic unicorn that appeared on its class rings for its mascot. The mythical animal was taken off the coat of arms of Prince Carl of Solms-Braunfels. It was later discovered that the animal on the coat of arms was actually a rampant blue lion on a gold field and not a unicorn. Described as half of an oval shield, the seal was cut off a bit lower at the top when the ring was designed, removing one of the lion's ears. The remaining ear appeared to be the horn of a unicorn.

The unicorn is the most noble and courageous of all beasts. He represents the finest qualities of the animal kingdom. His head of a horse signifies intelligence; his twisted horn, unity; his body of a lion, spirit and sportsmanship; and his feet of a deer, swiftness.

A jeweler's accident led to the creation of the only unicorn mascot in the state of Texas, and probably in the United States.

Wampus Cats
Itasca High School

The origin of the Itasca High School Wampus Cats is debatable among the residents of Itasca. According to a 1962 homecoming issue of the Itasca High School newspaper, the term *Wampus Cat* was created during the fall of 1921 at a school pep rally. During the ceremonies, a yell leader hollered out that one of the Itasca High School football players was a Wampus Cat, or a ferocious player. A few days later, the school decided that the entire football team should be named the Wampus Cats. The name stuck, and students created a huge black cat to represent this unique mascot.

Although this sounds like a logical explanation for this unusual team name, other legends trace the name Wampus Cat to the Cherokee Indian tribe. Cherokee folklore is filled with tales of evil spirits lurking in the deep, dark forests that surrounded their villages. But in areas of Georgia and Tennessee residents claim that there have been several Wampus Cat sightings in their towns. In southeastern Georgia, many people have reported hearing strange, high-pitched screams late at night and seeing a shaggy, man-like creature loping through the woods. In essence, the Wampus Cat is half man and half wildcat. In Tennessee, the Wampus Cat is described as a large, striped cat that is "about the size of a large spaniel."

The rumors are ongoing, but one question still remains: "Who created the Wampus Cat?" The answer is unknown, but a *San Antonio Express-News* article tied it to the residents of Itasca: "Wampus Cat - n., a fierce animal that does not exist other than in the hearts and minds of the people in the town of Itasca."

Warhorses
Devine High School

The dictionary defines *warhorse* as "a powerful horse—a charger—one who has had a stormy but successful career."

Since 1923, Devine High students, former students, and friends have worn the name Warhorse, rallying behind it to encourage each other to greater achievement in many situations. The great horse, known for its pride, strength, and endurance among horses, and standing for many of the qualities to which groups and individuals should aspire, has given long and loyal service. The name Warhorse has become synonymous with Devine High School; yet there was a time when there was no DHS Warhorse.

The story behind the tradition goes back to the 1923-24 school year. It was the year of the school's third football team. A young man named Robert Clyde Tate had come to DHS as a teacher and coach. The young coach had a nickname he had acquired during his college days —*Warhorse*.

During the 1923 football season, fans and foes alike formed the habit of referring to the determined, hard-working coach as Warhorse and Old Warhorse.

The football team was dubbed Warhorse's Boys. Later in the year, the team was faced with the decision of selecting an official nickname for itself. A 1923 *Whirlwind* (the DHS newspaper at the time) described the event, which occurred at a football banquet, in this way: "After much discussion, it was decided that in the future the Devine football team would be known as the Warhorses."

Whitefaces
Hereford High School

In Texas the cattle business is big, and knowing the different types of cattle ranks up there with knowing your state capitals. That's because Texans take pride in the foundations of the state—oil and gas, cowboys, horses, windstorms, and cattle. In Hereford it's no different.

Charles Goodnight of the JA Ranch of West Texas attempted to breed Durham (shorthorn) cattle but found that they were not suited to the environment and instead switched to Herefords. He introduced Herefords into the Panhandle in 1883 when he placed twenty registered bulls on the JA Ranch. The Hereford is a possible cross between red animals from Yorkshire and whitefaced animals from Holland, and the crossbreed sports a red body and white face.

The Hereford Independent School District acquired the defunct Hereford College buildings and six acres of campus for a new public school in 1915. As the town grew and the six acres were divided for public school use, the high school was compelled to find its own identity. From its original cross-functioning campus, it decided that these crossbred cattle were the perfect representation of its hometown pride and began calling itself the Hereford Whitefaces, or, in settings where ferocity is key, the Hostile Herd.

Wildcats
Westbury Christian School

Westbury Christian School was originally organized by a group of Abilene Christian University alumni. Borrowing the ACU mascot, the wildcat became the mascot for Westbury Christian School. Although the wildcat mascot does not have a name, it appears on the sidelines at football and home basketball games. In attempts at being friendly, the wildcat has frequently terrified small children. While it is not funny for the children, the mascot provides comedic entertainment for the rest of the crowd.

Yeguas
Somerville High School

Although the Spanish explorer Alonso De Leon named the heavily wooded creek that he discovered in 1690 (while checking out the land around the trail that became The Old San Antonio Road and much later Texas Highway 21) San Francisco, the name did not catch on. As time went by, other Spanish soldiers who traveled in the area called the creek the *Yegua*, a Spanish word that means mare or female horse. The creek was identified as River Yegua on a map of the area (that would become a part of Texas) by Stephen F. Austin. This map was published in New York in 1846. In later maps the creek was identified as Yegua Creek.

The reason the Spanish explorers called the creek Yegua or mare was that the Indian tribes that traveled through the area following the herds of buffalo would camp along the banks of the creek. The thickets, heavy growth of trees, and the other vegetation along the banks of the creek made a safe place for the Indians' mares to give birth and care for their foals until they were able to travel.

During the 1830s to 1850s, when early settlers started moving into the area that would become southern Burleson County (which is bordered by Yegua Creek), it is thought locally that stories about Yegua Indians were told around campfires. The fact that the word *yegua* meant mare in Spanish was not known in Somerville, Texas, until the 1950s or 1960s.

Somerville High School athletic teams are still proudly called the Somerville Yeguas and the Somerville Lady Yeguas.

Zebras
Grandview High School

Known as the Blue Bonnets from the 1800s until around 1921, Grandview High School is now the only school in the state of Texas with the zebra for its mascot. The old Blue Bonnet mascot did not refer to the state wildflower, but to a type of ladies' hat. The switch occurred around 1921, when new team uniforms were ordered. When the coach opened the box, he found that the uniforms were black and white striped. In a pinch, the team donned the striped jerseys and proudly pranced onto the field with the new moniker, Grandview Zebras. The name stuck, and they have been the Zebras ever since. Grandview's first live mascot was actually a donkey painted with black and white stripes. There are only seven other schools in the nation with zebra as their mascot.

THINGS THAT MAKE YOU GO *HMMMMM* . . .

"Texans for the most part have never learned how to be dull."

—Randolph B. Campbell

Buttons
Central Catholic High School

The expression "cute as a button" might not be applicable to the kind of button for which the Central Catholic High School mascot is named. Button is the term for each rattle in the end of a rattlesnake's tail. Opposing teams unaware of this meaning might find themselves suddenly taken by surprise by a team they thought was represented by a cute fastening fixture on a shirt.

Buttons as a mascot was derived from the former mascot, Rattlesnakes, as the result of a change in the school's name and location. Originally a part of St. Mary's College, founded in 1852, the high school was relocated in 1932 and the rattlesnake mascot was divided. According to their web site, St. Mary's University became the Rattlers and Central Catholic High School became the Buttons.

Marianist Brother Fred Halwe designed this picture to explain the difference between a Rattler and a Button. He now teaches at St. Mary's University.

Daisies
Hockaday High School

The Hockaday High School crest bears a unicorn, but in the 1980s the student council voted to adopt the Killer Daisy as a mascot. This stems from the nickname for students at Hockaday: Hockadaisies. Though there has been debate among the students to change the mascot over the past few years, it has remained unchanged.

Among their famous alumni are the twins Barbara and Jenna Bush, daughters of President George W. Bush and First Lady Laura Bush.

Maroons
Austin High School

Austin High loves its colors, so much so that they also serve as its mascot, along with an odd little creature known as Mr. Maroo, of indifferent appearance and origin but of enduring pride. From 1881 until the 1930s, Austin High had no "critter" mascot, and was known simply as the Maroons. In the '30s the school newspaper (called, you guessed it, the *Maroon*) recorded several efforts to create an animal mascot, but student votes in 1935 and '36 resulted in no clear decision. Ideas included something called the Flapdoodle in 1938 and a cheerleader-sweater-wearing Springer Spaniel puppy named Maroona in 1939, but there remained no official mascot.

Austin High resisted the idea that it needed a mascot until 1953, when two new high schools were built to meet the demands of the rising local population: McCallum and Travis. When faced with the question "What's a Maroon?" Austin High students defiantly answered that a *maroon* is someone who wears maroon —end of discussion. However, there was the idea of a character called *Mr. Maroo* or *L'il Maroo*, who first appeared in print in the September 20, 1957, *Maroon*, where the mascot (about 1.1 meters tall and hairy) is chasing the District Championship football trophy, outrunning district foes such as the McCallum Knights and the Temple Wildcats. At that time, the artist/creator/father of the mascot was Gilbert Reyes, a 1958 graduate of AHS.

There is a recurring legend that the mascot "fell to earth" as the "head of a comet" and some AHS students "found him and took care of him." Falling to earth would be consistent with Dogpatch origins—from a cartoon strip drawn by Al Capp—that Gilbert Reyes used. Reyes said he found that there were the schmoos—lovable friendly critters shaped like bowling pins, and then there were the *killer* schmoos—mean, nasty and hairy. Reyes says L'il Maroo was supposed to be a love child of a secret

Maroons
Austin High School
—Continued—

romance between one of each and thus a mutant, retaining the strong qualities of both. There was no known origin of the schmoos and killer schmoos "on earth." Al Capp, the artist of *L'il Abner*, said they came from the "Valley of the Schmoon."

Mighty Mites
Masonic Home and School

Norman Strange and Miller Moseley, who graduated from the Masonic Home and School in 1939, still remember the day the school acquired its mascot. Norman Strange is a retired CPA who owned his own firm for forty years; in fact, his firm audited the Masonic Home and School until he retired. Dr. Miller Moseley is now a retired professor from TCU.

It all started in 1938, when their football team went to the semifinals against Lubbock High. The majority of Masonic Home and School's team didn't weigh more than 165 pounds each. According to a writer from the *Fort Worth Press*, "They were small but mighty," and according to Norman, that name has stuck ever since. The very next year, he and Miller started as offensive ends for the Masonic Mighty Mites.

Rockets
Irvin High School

Irvin High School was built when 98% of the population was military. The military primarily did rocketing, so the school mascot is the Rockets. The patriotic colors of red, white, and blue were chosen by the coaches and school board to represent Irvin pride. Irvin saw some more physical changes in 1998. While Irvin has always had a Rocketman team mascot, 2001 was the first year it included a Rocketwoman. It resurrected its spirit club, the Rocketteers, in 2001. The club members show their Rocket pride by decorating the parking lot before football games and organizing parties, projects, workshops, and gatherings.

Sandies
Amarillo High School

Amarillo High School, founded in the late 1800s, transitioned from a two room county courthouse to a downtown city hall building that was also home to donkeys and horses not suitable for the ever-growing student body. It wasn't until 1921 that a new building was built to accommodate the rising student population. It's no wonder, with students being overcrowded and overrun by four-legged creatures, that the school mascot was the Savage.

Perhaps the Amarillo High student body felt that the name Savages hadn't brought them any luck, or perhaps they were just ahead of their time in complying with modern-day political correctness; whatever the reason, they decided that a new mascot was in order. During a windy baseball practice in 1922, a new mascot was born. The school's history states that through the windblown sand rising from the field, the baseball coach yelled at the players, "Come on, you golden sandstormers, come on now, bear down." Soon after, the name "Golden Sandstorm" took hold. From that year forward, the then-retired Amarillo Savages became known by the newly christened nickname Sandies. Sandie himself has received many facelifts over the years, just as the school itself has undergone many changes. The building built for the growing population in 1921 was tragically destroyed by a fire in 1970 and rebuilt in a new location across town. Considering the track record of this school, it is odd that the Phoenix was never suggested as a mascot option.

Whirlwinds
Floydada High School

Never underestimate the power of a good newspaper article. One day in the 1920s the Floydada football team played the Amarillo Sandies. They came in and out like a whirlwind, according to what the Amarillo paper said the next day. The name stuck, and the Floydada mascot has been the Whirlwinds ever since.

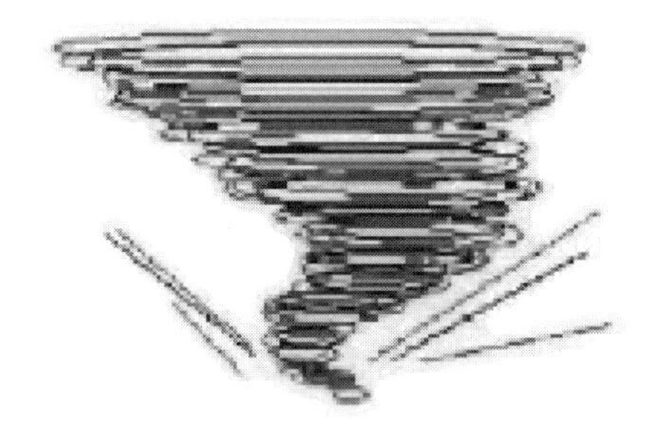

Chapter 3

What Else Would They Be Called?
The Obvious Mascot Names

"If you can't make it better, you can laugh at it."
—Erma Louise Bombeck

Welcome to Muleshoe, Home of the Mules
Restating the Obvious

This chapter is dedicated to those Texas high schools that didn't have any alternative when it came to picking a mascot. Their choices were just too obvious to be overlooked. Consider the student from Buffalo, Texas, who attends Buffalo High School. What point could there possibly be in confusing the rest of the state by naming his mascot the Broncos? None—exactly. The Buffalo High School student body did the right thing: It adopted the bison as its mascot.

White Deer High School in White Deer also followed this rule of thumb and called itself the Bucks. This, however, begs the question: What does it call its female athletes? The Buckettes? The Buckets? Or are they more aptly referred to as the Doe? And, on any playing field from a volleyball court to a chessboard, the loyal fans from Elkhart High School will be cheering for . . . the Elks! And there are the Deer Park High School Deer and the Hereford Herd.

Before leaving this animal section, the Wolfe City Wolves definitely deserve a mention. Another aptly named critter is the Tom Bean Tomcat. Here, too, one has to wonder what its female athletes go by. Let's just leave that one to our imaginations. Now, say Itasca Cats three times as fast as you can and you too may sound like you're coughing up a hairball. What other mascot could they have chosen? Actually, neither of these school's cats is the cuddly type. They are big ferocious cats. Itasca's cat, for example, is the Wampus Cat, which looks a lot like a very hungry tiger.

The blue-ribbon award winner in the critter section has to be the Mesquite Skeeters. This school clearly had only one option. Perhaps it could have picked the mesquite tree with its sharp thorns, 100-year life expectancy, and flavor enhancement that makes Texas barbecue the best in the world. But, the Skeeter is the wiser choice: much faster and more elusive.

The Crane High School mascot is the Crane! Students who live in Eagle Pass and attend the high school of the same name—you can bet your feathers that they'll be cheering for Old Baldy. That's right, without question, they're the Eagles. Other birds worth mentioning are the Hawkins Hawks from Hawkins and the Birdville High School Hawks.

The Fighting Farmers are, of course, residents of Farmersville. That might serve as fodder for an all-out turf war. What is the difference between Plains and Happy Cowboys? Their hometowns—Plains and Happy! Is either team capable of rounding up the Hereford High School Herd? Or are they more closely matched up with the Muleshoe Mules?

Two high schools in the Houston area, when faced with the challenge of whether or not to go with the obvious mascot, jumped on the bandwagon. Generals lead both schools through their battles. What are the schools in question? Robert E. Lee and Douglas B. MacArthur. This is probably the best place in this chapter to include San Antonio's Roosevelt Rough Riders.

Neither Roma High School on the outskirts of Dallas nor Italy High School deep in the Rio Grande Valley could resist their destiny—they did not hesitate to adopt the Gladiators as their mascots. Here's hoping that these two schools someday make it to a state tournament and have the opportunity to battle to the death! This seems highly unlikely, however, should either team do battle with the Albany, Blooming Grove, Brownwood, Turner, Dublin, Clint, Ennis, Castleberry, Franklin, Union Grove, Greenville, Henderson, Taylor, Yates, Kaufman, Kenedy, Kountze, La Feria, Leander, Livingston, Lockhart, Lovelady, McKinney, New Boston, New Deal, Ozona, Ponder, Roby, Roxton, Spring, Teague, John Tyler, Vernon, Waco, Cranfills Gap, or Lutheran High North *Lions* along the way.

This makes one wonder what happened to the students in Athens? Why did they settle on the Hornets when they should have been the Spartans? Probably because they didn't want to make this list of the obvious! The Troy High School Trojans, on the other hand, fell right into place.

Several other Texas high schools have made an obvious choice by using weather phenomena to capitalize on the name of their towns or regions. Where is Winters, Texas? Do you suppose they really have blizzards there? Well they do now. Every time one of their teams takes the playing field, the locals are screaming for Blizzards. As for the Amarillo Golden Sandstorm, there's no mystery there. Central High School in Fort Worth has chosen to be called the Lightning Bolts. True, there is no apparent reason for this one, since lightning has been known to strike in every part of the state, but it was an interesting choice. Maybe there was a big thunderstorm outside the day they had to choose. Also worthy of mention are the Lamesa Tornadoes and the Floydada Whirlwinds.

So far the school mascots examined have all been pretty obvious choices. However, in today's *politically correct* society, where it has become more acceptable to rewrite history than to acknowledge it, one has to wonder why the students of Robert E. Lee High School in Midland still call their mascot the Rebels. Don't they know it's better to pretend that the Civil War never happened? They should consider changing not only the mascot but also the name of the school. Modernize—call them the Midlanders. Keep up with the times. Consider a more contemporary statesman to inspire a mascot. For example, the William Jefferson Clinton *Interns* or the George W. Bush *Guardsmen* would be more politically acceptable, and both mascot names are probably still available.

Add to this category of politically incorrect schools that had no other choice than to become either the Indians or a specific tribe. Legend has it that a Texas Ranger named the City of Nacona after Peta Nocona, a chief of the Comanche—therefore the Nocona Indians. Quanah, also named for a Comanche chief, Quanah Parker, adopted the Indian as a mascot. And, who can blame the student residents of Seminole, Texas, for wanting to be hailed as the Seminole Indians? As one can see, the problem of political compliance here runs even deeper. These poor folks may have to change the names of their towns too!

Naming a parochial school mascot also carries a heavy burden—how to be "holier than thou" but still provoke fear in one's competitors. Concordia Lutheran High School, Northeast Christian Academy, Strake Jesuit College Preparatory, and Sweetwater Christian School probably made the best decision in that dilemma by picking the obvious: the *Crusaders*. And those Catholics from

Cathedral High School had no choice but to go with the Fighting Irish. Baytown Christian Academy and Harvest Christian Academy may, however, be carrying things a bit too far by calling themselves the Saints.

Here is another unwritten but apparently mandatory rule: If a high school is located in the Gulf Coast area, a ferocious game fish must serve as the mascot. But which one? Are one's odds better against the Port Aransas Marlins, the Austwell-Tivoli Redfish, the Palacios or Sachse Sharks, or the Port Isabel Fighting Tarpons?

Yet another mascot option for schools in Texas is to tout the local livelihood. Examples of these include the Brazosport High School Exporters in Freeport and the Pearland High School Oilers, not to mention the Robstown Cottonpickers.

Rider High School in Wichita Falls deserves special mention in this chapter for laziness if nothing else in sticking with the obvious in choosing the Raiders. There should be little fear of forgetting that one. What is it again? Oh yeah, just add a letter! And the Cameron Yoe Yoemen—what is a *Yoeman* anyway? Well, it beats the heck out of the Yoe-Yoes!

However, an all-time favorite and Grand Prize Winner has to be the Hamlin High School *Pied Pipers*. What more can be said?

So, the next time you're taking a road trip through Texas, don't be too surprised when you're speeding through a small town and encounter a billboard proclaiming *Welcome to Muleshoe, Home of the Mules*! Slow down, pull over, and cheer them on!

Chapter 4

Politically Incorrect

"The thing about Texas is, it's where all of these cultures—Anglo, Tejano, and American Indian cultures meet."

—Thomas Knowles

Offensive-Defensive

Schools adopt mascots to represent a spirit, a symbol, or an image. However, some mascots are found to be offensive because of racial stereotyping. Native American activists around the country are protesting Indian mascots used by schools. The campaign to challenge mascots began in the late 1960s and continues today. Along with Indian mascots, protesters want tokens, nicknames, logos, and other associated symbols changed. The reason the groups want change is that they feel the images are negative stereotypes, often depicting Native Americans as cruel and savage. Cartoon-like imagery tends to dehumanize, they say, thereby reducing the group to a subhuman level.

Mascots fall into several categories: animals, acts of nature, professions, and race. It is the last category in which the Indian mascot falls. Many schools feel that they are honoring Native Americans by adopting Indian-related mascots such as Redskins, Warriors, Chiefs, Savages, Apaches, or Braves. The question protesters ask is this: If the people being "honored" feel only degradation, pain, racism, and disgust, then where is the honor?

Struggles have arisen not only over racial mascots, but over history and power. Traditionalists don't want change. Protesters won't back down. And at some schools the Confederate flag still waves. Against the backdrop of the civil rights movement, the Confederate flag gained renewed importance throughout the Deep South, symbolizing Southern nationalism. To some, the Confederate flag represents the fight over slavery and white supremacy. Therefore, schools with the rebel mascot or with Confederate generals as mascots are confronted with changing their images.

The rebel mascot is often depicted as the cartoon character, Yosemite Sam. Rather than change their rebel mascot, some schools have merely eliminated hoisting the Confederate flag or substituted a school flag. Some schools have removed offensive mascots and replaced them with something else. Others are hanging onto their traditions.

Politically Correct Mascots & Lawsuits

Although many individuals and organizations have protested controversial mascots, no Texas school district has been sued for the unlawful use of a school mascot, according to a recent article in the *Texas Association of School Boards.* However, there have been many notable cases in which an offended party has threatened legal action. In 2001, the San Antonio American Indian Resource Center threatened to file lawsuits against the Harlandale and Jourdanton school districts in San Antonio because they refused to change their Indian mascots and team names. Jonathan Hook, the president of San Antonio's American Indian Resource Center, visited four San Antonio school districts to explain how Indian mascots are offensive and asked that the Harlandale, Jourdanton, North East, and San Antonio school districts change the names. Both the North East and San Antonio districts complied with the organization's wishes. (Information quoted from the San Antonio Associate Press Bureau. The article was printed in the *Abilene Reporter-News*).

In April, 2001, the Alvarado Independent School District faced the threat of legal action when a local high school student complained that the use of Indian mascots was discriminating and offensive. A Johnson County teenager stirred up the controversy when she wrote the Alvarado ISD superintendent and asked him to change the Indian mascot. Superintendent Ben Colwell said that the Indian was a tribute to Indian heritage and represented "honor, nobility, strength and courage," and he did not change the name. The controversy was referred to the Texas Education Agency, which replied that the agency could not regulate mascots; however, the agency would respond if formal hearings were not set up to allow concerned residents to voice their opinions about the use of an Indian mascot. A school board hearing was held in May, and several people came to voice their opinions, including a Native American woman from Washington. In the end, the school decided to keep the Indian mascot.

Chapter 5

Mascot Gallery

"It's not the size of the dog in the fight,
it's the size of the fight in the dog."
—Mark Twain

Bastrop High School
Bears

Aubrey High School
Chaparrals

Bangs High School
Dragons

Bridge City High School
Cardinals

Denton High School
Broncos

Dumas High School
Demons

Falls City High School
Beavers

Merkel High School
Badgers

Mexia High School
Blackcats

Poteet High School
Aggies

South Garland High School
Colonels

Knippa High School
Rockcrushers

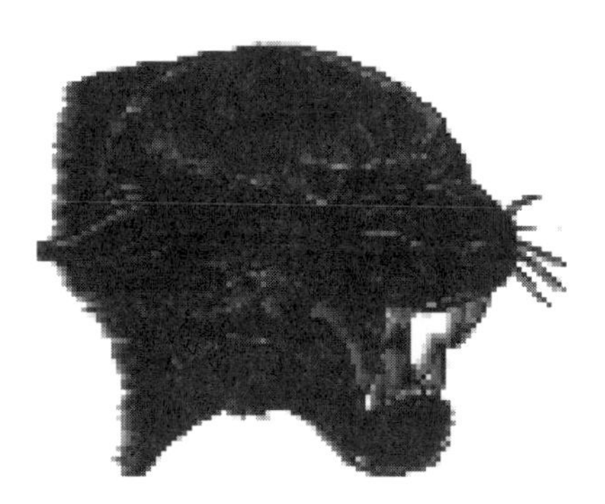

Caney Creek High School
Panthers

Churchill High School
Chargers

Lyford Consolidated High School
Bulldogs

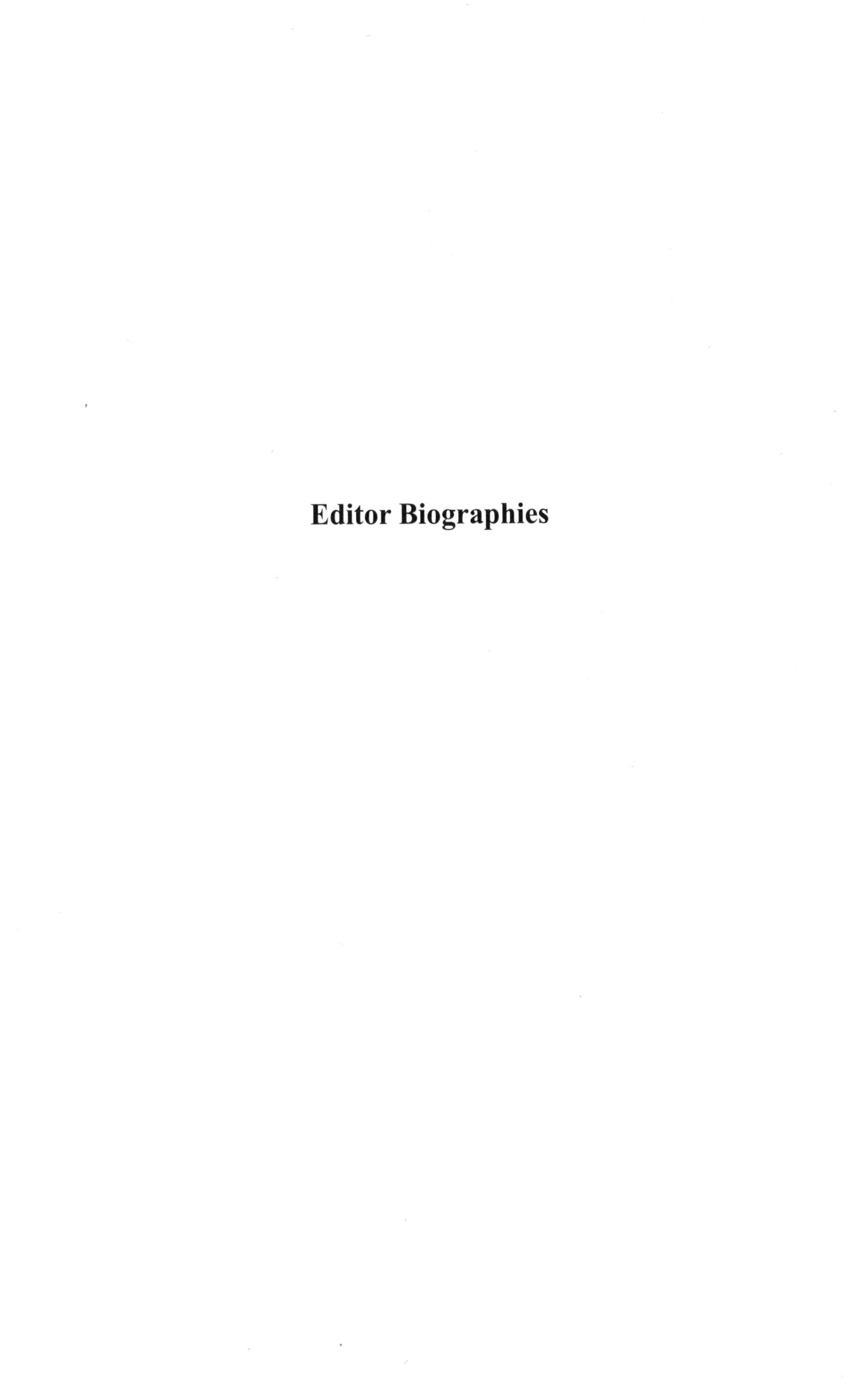

Editor Biographies

Editor Biographies

Sabrina Barlow is a graduate student in the Master of Arts-English program at Sam Houston State University. She earned a Bachelor of Science Degree in Dance with a minor in art from Texas Woman's University before pursuing a career as a performing artist and professional choreographer. She also holds a Texas real estate broker's license. Sabrina plans to graduate from the English program in August 2005. She attended Denton High School in Denton, Texas, home of the Broncos.

Betty Burdett is currently pursuing a Master of Arts degree in English with a minor in Adult Literacy at Sam Houston State University. She earned a Bachelor of Arts degree in English from Sam Houston State University before she began her current career as a temporary full-time professor of Developmental Studies (both reading and writing) at Tomball College, a community college in Tomball, Texas. Although Betty has held several corporate positions in association management, including Executive Director of the Petroleum Industry Security Council, she says that her greatest achievement has been successfully raising her two adult daughters. Betty attended Stephen F. Austin High School in Austin, home of one of the most unusual mascots in this book—Mr. Maroo.

Damien Carey is an English major at Sam Houston State University. He currently works as a writer and consultant and hopes to pursue a career as a novelist after graduating in 2006. Damien graduated from Cardinal Mooney High School in Youngstown, Ohio, home of the Cardinals.

Urania Fung is a graduate student pursuing a Master of Arts degree in English at Sam Houston State University. She earned a Bachelor of Science degree in computer science from the University of Texas at Austin before pursuing a career as an English teacher in China. After graduating in May 2006, Urania plans to pursue a Ph.D. in English at a major university. She is a graduate of Lamar High School in Arlington, home of the Vikings.

Patricia Healy is a graduate student pursuing a Master of Arts degree in English-Creative Writing at Sam Houston State University. She earned a B.B.A. in Petroleum Land Management from the University of Texas at Austin before pursuing careers as a landman and professional journalist. In addition to reporting for *Petroleum News Alaska*, a weekly newspaper in Anchorage, Patricia has also worked as a freelance writer for the *Houston Chronicle* and *Alaska Parenting*. After graduating from Sam Houston State University in December 2005, Patricia hopes to write and publish a book. She graduated from Cy-Fair High School in Cypress, Texas, home of the Bobcats.

Tamara Hill is a graduate student pursuing a Master of Arts degree in English-Creative Writing at Sam Houston State University. She earned a Bachelor of Science degree in Mass Communications from Texas Woman's University before pursuing a career in print and broadcast journalism. Tamara worked as a health reporter and columnist for the *Corpus Christi Caller-Times* and later pursued careers in corporate communications and public relations. After graduating in December 2005, Tamara hopes to continue teaching writing courses at a community college and to publish a monthly magazine. She graduated from DeSoto High School in DeSoto, Texas, home of the Eagles.

Amanda Huffer is currently pursuing a Master of Arts degree in English with an emphasis in Creative Writing at Sam Houston State University. She earned a Bachelors Degree in English from Sam Houston State University before she began her current career as an English teacher at Caney Creek High School in Conroe, Texas. Although Amanda held many high-stress corporate positions for eleven years before her pursuit of teaching and writing, she says that her most challenging, yet most rewarding job is being a mom to her four young children. Amanda attended Klein Oak High School in Spring, Texas, home of the Panthers. From the Klein Oak Panthers to the Caney Creek Panthers, she just can't seem to get away from that mascot!

Kelly Rowan is a graduate student pursuing a Master of Arts degree in English at Sam Houston State University. She earned a Bachelor's Degree in English and double minors in philosophy and art history from Sam Houston State University in 2003. After graduating with her Master's degree in August 2005, Kelly hopes to pursue a career in education, teaching at either the high school or junior college level. She graduated from Victoria High School in Victoria, Texas, home of the Stingarees. Note: After a recent merger of two rival high schools in Victoria, Victoria High School changed its name and mascot to Memorial High School, home of the Vipers.

Christina Tonan is a graduate student pursuing a Master of Arts degree in English-Creative Writing at Sam Houston State University. This California native earned a Bachelor of Science Degree in Finance from California State University at Long Beach (CSULB) and has earned two teaching credentials since. Christina worked in elementary education for eight years as a second grade teacher and reading specialist. She is a member of the South Basin Writing Project and spends summers as a writing consultant for CSULB. After relocating to Texas, she taught reading and writing at Tomball College. Upon her graduation in December 2005, Christina hopes to write, teach, and take art classes while putting her son William through college. Christina attended Downey High School in Downey, California, home of the Vikings.

Gary Charles Wilkens is pursuing a Master of Arts Degree in English at Sam Houston State University. He earned a Bachelor of Arts degree in philosophy from Hendrix College in Conway, Arkansas, before moving to Germany to marry and work as an English tutor. After graduating from Sam Houston State University in December 2005, Gary plans to pursue a career as a professional poet and professor of creative writing. He is already an accomplished poet, whose work has appeared in or will soon appear in *The Adirondack Review*, *The Texas Review*, *The Taj Mahal Review*, *The God Particle, Remark*, and *Clean Sheets*. Gary graduated from Fayetteville High School in Fayetteville, Arkansas, home of the Bulldogs.

Dan Sellers is a graduate student in the Master of Arts program in English at Sam Houston State and Assistant Director of Texas Review Press. He holds a Bachelor of Arts degree in sociology and history from Western Kenturcky State University and is a licensed aircraft mechanic. Dan has worked for several private, state, and federal agencies, including a position with the Royal Afghan Housing Authority. At various times he has been a Redskin, Bearkat, Hilltopper, Wildcat, and Cadet.

Dr. Paul Ruffin is the creative director and supervisor of the *Mascot Mania* project. He is Regents Distinguished Professor of English at Sam Houston State University, where he edits *The Texas Review* and directs the Texas Review Press (a member of the Texas A&M University Press Consortium). Dr. Ruffin is a critically acclaimed author who has published two novels, two collections of stories, and five collections of poetry, and he has edited or coedited eleven books. He also writes a weekly column that appears in several newspapers in Texas, Alabama, and Mississippi. His work has been featured nationally in magazines, journals, anthologies, and major university texts and on National Public Radio. His fourth collection of poetry, *Circling*, won the Mississippi Institute of Arts and Letters Poetry Prize in 1997. The *Dictionary of Literary Biography Yearbook* has cited his second collection of stories, *Islands, Women, and God*, as one of the best books of short stories published in America in 2001 and listed *Pompeii Man* as an Outstanding American Novel for 2002. His latest novel, *Castle in the Gloom*, was recently pubished by Univeristy Press of Mississippi, and his next book, *Here's to Noah, Bless His Ark and Other Musings*, will appear in the spring of 2005. Over the past three years, he has been a featured author at several events, including the Texas Book Festival, Eudora Welty Symposium, Tennessee Williams Symposium, and Southern Festival of Books. Dr. Ruffin graduated from Lee High School in Columbus, Mississippi, home of the Generals.

Index of Texas High School Mascots

Sorted by City

High School	Town	Mascot
	ABERNATHY	
Abernathy H.S.		Antelope
	ABILENE	
Abilene H.S.		Eagles
Cooper H.S.		Cougars
Wylie H.S.		Bulldogs
	AGUA DULCE	
Agua Dulce H.S.		Longhorns
	ALAMO	
PSJA Memorial H.S.		Wolverines
	ALBA	
Alba-Golden H.S.		Panthers
	ALBANY	
Albany Jr./Sr. H.S.		Lions
	ALEDO	
Aledo H.S.		Bearcats
	ALICE	
Alice H.S.		Coyotes
	ALLEN	
Allen H.S.		Eagles
	ALPINE	
Alpine H.S.		Fighting Bucks
	ALTAIR	
Rice H.S.		Raiders
	ALTO	
Alto H.S.		Yellow Jackets
	ALVARADO	
Alvarado H.S.		Indians
	ALVIN	
Alvin H.S.		Yellow Jackets
	ALVORD	
Alvord H.S.		Bulldogs
	AMARILLO	
Amarillo H.S.		Golden Sand-storm
Caprock H.S.		Longhorns
Highland Park H.S.		Hornets
Palo Duro H.S.		Dons

High School	Town	Mascot
	AMARILLO (Cont.)	
Randall H.S.		Raiders
River Road H.S.		Wildcats
Tascosa H.S.		Rebels
	ANAHUAC	
Anahuac H.S.		Panthers
	ANDREWS	
Andrews H.S.		Mustangs
	ANGLETON	
Angleton H.S.		Wildcats
	ANNA	
Anna H.S.		Coyotes
	ANSON	
Anson H.S.		Tigers
	ANTHONY	
Anthony H.S.		Wildcats
	ANTON	
Anton H.S.		Bulldogs
	APPLE SPRINGS	
Apple Springs H.S.		Eagles
	ARANSAS PASS	
Aransas Pass H.S.		Panthers
	ARCHER CITY	
Archer City H.S.		Wildcats
	ARGYLE	
Argyle H.S.		Eagles
	ARLINGTON	
Arlington H.S.		Colts
Bowie H.S.		Volunteers
Lamar H.S.		Vikings
Mansfield Timberview H.S.		Wolves
Martin H.S.		Warriors
Sam Houston H.S.		Texans
Seguin H.S.		Cougars
Summit H.S.		Jaguars
	ARP	
Arp H.S.		Tigers

High School	Town	Mascot
	ASPERMONT	
Aspermont H.S.		Hornets
	ATHENS	
Athens H.S.		Hornets
	ATLANTA	
Atlanta H.S.		Rabbits
	AUBREY	
Aubrey H.S.		Chaparrals
	AUSTIN	
Akins H.S.		Eagles
Anderson H.S.		Trojans
Austin H.S.		Maroons
Bowie H.S.		Bulldogs
Crockett H.S.		Cougars
Gonzalo Garza Ind. H.S.		Griffins
John B. Connally H.S.		no mascot
Johnson H.S.		Jaguars
Johnston H.S.		Rams
Lake Travis H.S.		Cavaliers
Lanier H.S.		Vikings
McCallum H.S.		Knights
McNeil H.S.		Mavericks
Reagan H.S.		Raiders
Travis H.S.		Rebels
UT at Austin H.S.		No mascot
Westlake H.S.		Chaparrals
Westwood H.S.		Warriors
	AVERY	
Avery H.S.		Bulldogs
	AVINGER	
Avinger H.S.		Bulldogs
	AVOCA	
Lueders-Avoca H.S.		no mascot
	AXTELL	
Axtell H.S.		Longhorns
	AZLE	
Azle H.S.		Hornets
	BAIRD	
Baird H.S.		Bears
	BALLINGER	
Ballinger H.S.		Bearcats

High School	Town	Mascot
	BANDERA	
Bandera H.S.		Bulldogs
	BANGS	
Bangs H.S.		Dragons
	BANQUETE	
Banquete H.S.		Bulldogs
	BARKSDALE	
Nueces Canyon J.H./H.S.		Panthers
	BARTLETT	
Bartlett H.S.		Bulldogs
	BASTROP	
Bastrop H.S.		Bears
	BAY CITY	
Bay City H.S.		Black Cats
	BAYTOWN	
Lee H.S.		Ganders
Sterling H.S.		Rangers
	BEAUMONT	
Central Senior H.S.		Jaguars
Monsignor Kelly H.S.		Bulldogs
Ozen H.S.		no mascot
West Brook Sr H.S.		Bruins
	BECKVILLE	
Beckville J.H./H.S.		Bearcats
	BEEVILLE	
A.C. Jones H.S.		Trojans
	BELLAIRE	
Bellaire H.S.		Cardinals
	BELLS	
Bells H.S.		Panthers
	BELLVILLE	
Bellville H.S.		Brahmas
	BELTON	
Belton H.S.		Tigers
Henry T. Waskow H.S.		Rangers
	BEN BOLT	
Ben Bolt-Pal Blanco H.S.		Badgers

High School	Town	Mascot
	BEN WHEELER	
Martins Mill H.S.		Mustangs
	BIG LAKE	
Reagan County H.S.		Owls
	BIG SANDY	
Big Sandy H.S.		Wildcats
Harmony H.S.		Eagles
	BIG SPRING	
Big Spring H.S.		Steers
	BISHOP	
Bishop H.S.		Badgers
	BLANCO	
Blanco H.S.		Panthers
	BLANKET	
Blanket H.S.		Tigers
	BLOOMBURG	
Bloomburg H.S.		Wildcats
	BLOOMING GROVE	
Blooming Grove H.S.		Lions
	BLOOMINGTON	
Bloomington H.S.		Bobcats
	BLUE RIDGE	
Blue Ridge H.S.		Tigers
	BOERNE	
Boerne H.S.		Greyhounds
	BOGATA	
Rivercrest H.S.		Rebels
	BOLING	
Boling H.S.		Bulldogs
	BONHAM	
Bonham H.S.		Purple Warriors
	BORGER	
Borger H.S.		Bulldogs
	BOVINA	
Bovina H.S.		Mustangs

High School	Town	Mascot
	BOWIE	
Bowie H.S.		Bears
	BOYD	
Boyd H.S.		Yellow Jackets
	BOYS RANCH	
Boys Ranch H.S.		Roughriders
	BRACKETTVILLE	
Brackett H.S.		Tigers
	BRADY	
Brady H.S.		Bulldogs
	BRECKENRIDGE	
Breckenridge H.S.		Buckaroos
	BREMOND	
Bremond H.S.		Fighting Tigers
	BRENHAM	
Brenham H.S.		Cubs
	BRIDGE CITY	
Bridge City H.S.		Cardinals
	BRIDGEPORT	
Bridgeport H.S.		Bulls
	BROADDUS	
Broaddus H.S.		Bulldogs
	BROCK	
Brock H.S.		Eagles
	BRONTE	
Bronte H.S.		Longhorns
	BROOKELAND	
Brookeland H.S.		Wildcats
	BROOKESMITH	
Brookesmith H.S.		Mustangs
	BROWNFIELD	
Brownfield H.S.		Cubs
	BROWNSBORO	
Brownsboro H.S.		Bears

High School	Town	Mascot
	BROWNSVILLE	
Hanna H.S.		Golden Eagles
Lopez H.S.		Lobos
Pace H.S.		Vikings
Porter H.S.		Fighting Cowboys
Rivera H.S.		Raiders
Valley Christian H.S.		no mascot
	BROWNWOOD	
Brownwood H.S.		Lions
	BRUNI	
Bruni H.S.		Badgers
	BRYAN	
Bryan H.S.		Vikings
	BUDA	
Jack C. Hays H.S.		Rebels
	BUFFALO	
Buffalo H.S.		Bison
	BULLARD	
Bullard H.S.		Panthers
	BUNA	
Buna H.S.		Cougars
	BURKBURNETT	
Burkburnett H.S.		Bulldogs
	BURKEVILLE	
Burkeville Jr./Sr. H.S.		Mustangs
	BURLESON	
Burleson H.S.		Elks
	BURNET	
Burnet H.S.		Bulldogs
	BURTON	
Burton H.S.		Panthers
	BUSHLAND	
Bushland H.S.		Falcons
	CADDO MILLS	
Caddo Mills H.S.		Foxes
	CALDWELL	
Caldwell H.S.		Hornets

High School	Town	Mascot
	CALVERT	
Calvert H.S.		Trojans
	CAMERON	
Yoe H.S.		Yoemen
	CAMPBELL	
Campbell H.S.		Indians
	CANADIAN	
Canadian H.S.		Wildcats
	CANTON	
Canton H.S.		Eagles
	CANUTILLO	
Canutillo H.S.		Eagles
	CANYON	
Canyon H.S.		Eagles
	CARMINE	
Round Top-Carmine		Cubs
	CARRIZO SPRINGS	
Carrizo Springs H.S.		Wildcats
	CARROLLTON	
Creekview H.S.		Mustangs
Hebron H.S.		Hawks
Smith H.S.		Trojans
Turner H.S.		Lions
	CARTHAGE	
Carthage H.S.		Bulldogs
	CASTROVILLE	
Medina Valley H.S.		Panthers
	CAYUGA	
Cayuga H.S.		Wildcats
	CEDAR PARK	
Cedar Park H.S.		Timber Wolves
	CEDAR HILL	
Cedar Hill H.S.		Longhorns
	CELESTE	
Celeste H.S.		Blue Devils

Town / High School	Mascot
CELINA	
Celina H.S.	Bobcats
CENTER	
Center H.S.	Roughriders
CENTER POINT	
Center Point H.S.	Pirates
CENTERVILLE	
Centerville Jr/Sr H.S.	Tigers
CHANNELVIEW	
Channelview H.S.	Falcons
CHARLOTTE	
Charlotte H.S.	Trojans
CHEROKEE	
Cherokee H.S.	Indians
CHICO	
Chico H.S.	Dragons
CHILDRESS	
Childress H.S.	Bobcats
CHILLICOTHE	
Chillicothe H.S.	Eagles
CHINA SPRING	
China Spring H.S.	Cougars
CHIRENO	
Chireno H.S.	Owls
CIBOLO	
Byron P. Steele II H.S.	no mascot
CISCO	
Cisco H.S.	Lobos
CLARENDON	
Clarendon H.S.	Broncos
CLARKSVILLE	
Clarksville H.S.	Tigers
CLEBURNE	
Cleburne H.S.	Yellow Jackets
CLEVELAND	
Cleveland H.S.	Indians
Tarkington H.S.	Longhorns

Town / High School	Mascot
CLIFTON	
Clifton H.S.	Cubs
CLYDE	
Clyde H.S.	Bulldogs
Eula H.S.	Pirates
COAHOMA	
Coahoma H.S.	Bulldogs
COLDSPRING	
Coldspring-Oakhurst H.S.	Trojans
COLEMAN	
Coleman H.S.	Blue Cats
COLLEGE STATION	
A & M Consolidated H.S.	Tigers
COLLEYVILLE	
Colleyville Heritage H.S.	Panthers
COLLINSVILLE	
Collinsville H.S.	Pirates
COLMESNEIL	
Colmesneil H.S.	Bulldogs
COLORADO CITY	
Colorado H.S.	Wolves
COLUMBUS	
Columbus H.S.	Cardinals
COMANCHE	
Comanche H.S.	Indians
COMFORT	
Comfort H.S.	Bobcats
COMMERCE	
Commerce H.S.	Tigers
CONROE	
Academy of Science	no mascot
Caney Creek H.S.	Panthers
Conroe H.S.	Tigers
Oak Ridge H.S.	Eagles
The Woodlands H.S.	Highlanders
CONVERSE	
Judson H.S.	Rockets

High School	Town	Mascot
	COOPER	
Cooper H.S.		Bulldogs
	COPPELL	
Coppell H.S.		Cowboys
	COPPERAS COVE	
Copperas Cove H.S.		Bulldogs
	CORPUS CHRISTI	
Calallen H.S.		Wildcats
Carroll H.S.		Tigers
Flour Bluff H.S.		Hornets
Incarnate Word H.S.		Angels
King H.S.		Mustangs
Moody H.S.		Trojans
New H.S.		No mascot
Ray H.S.		Fighting Texans
Tuloso-Midway H.S.		Warriors
West Oso H.S.		Bears
	CORRIGAN	
Corrigan-Camden H.S.		Bulldogs
	CORSICANA	
Corsicana H.S.		Tigers
Mildred H.S.		Eagles
	COTULLA	
Cotulla H.S.		Cowboys
	CRANDALL	
Crandall H.S.		Pirates
	CRANE	
Crane H.S.		Cranes
	CRAWFORD	
Crawford H.S.		Pirates
	CROCKETT	
Crockett H.S.		Bulldogs
	CROSBY	
Crosby H.S.		Cougars
	CROSBYTON	
Crosbyton H.S.		Chiefs
	CROSS PLAINS	
Cross Plains H.S.		Buffaloes
	CROWELL	
Crowell H.S.		Wildcats
	CROWLEY	
Crowley H.S.		Eagles
	CRYSTAL CITY	
Crystal City H.S.		Javelinas
	CUERO	
Cuero H.S.		Gobblers
	CUMBY	
Cumby H.S.		Trojans
	CYPRESS	
Cy-Fair H.S.		Bobcats
Cypress Springs H.S.		Panthers
	DAINGERFIELD	
Daingerfield H.S.		Tigers
	DAISETTA	
Hull-Daisetta H.S.		no mascot
	DALHART	
Dalhart H.S.		Golden Wolves
	DALLAS	
A. Maceo Smith H.S.		Falcons
Barbara Manns H.S.		Night Hawks
Bryan Adams H.S.		Cougars
David W. Carter H.S.		Cowboys
H. Grady Spruce H.S.		Timber Wolves
Highland Park H.S.		Scots
Hillcrest H.S.		Panthers
James Madison H.S.		Trojans
Justin F. Kimball H.S.		Knights
L.G. Pinkston H.S.		Vikings
Lake Highlands H.S.		Wildcats
Lincoln H.S.		Tigers
Moises Molina H.S.		Jaguars
North Dallas H.S.		Bulldogs
Roosevelt H.S.		Mustangs
Skyline H.S.		Raiders
South Oak Cliff H.S.		Bears
Sunset H.S.		Bison
Thomas Jefferson H.S.		Patriots
W.H. Adamson H.S.		Leopards
W.T. White H.S.		Longhorns

High School	Town	Mascot
	DALLAS (Cont'd)	
W.W. Samuell H.S.		Spartans
Wilmer-Hutchins H.S.		Eagles
Woodrow Wilson H.S.		Wildcats
	DANBURY	
Danbury H.S.		Panthers
	DAYTON	
Dayton H.S.		Broncos
	DE LEON	
De Leon H.S.		Bearcats
	DECATUR	
Cates H.S.		no mascot
Decatur H.S.		Eagles
	DEER PARK	
Deer Park H.S.		Deer
	DEKALB	
Dekalb H.S.		Bears
	DEL RIO	
Del Rio H.S.		Rams
	DEL VALLE	
Del Valle H.S.		Cardinals
	DENISON	
Denison H.S.		Yellow Jackets
	DENTON	
Denton H.S.		Broncos
Fred Moore H.S.		no mascot
John H. Guyer H.S.		no mascot
Ryan H.S.		Broncos
	DENVER CITY	
Denver City H.S.		Mustangs
	DE SOTO	
De Soto H.S.		Eagles
	DETROIT	
Detroit H.S.		Eagles
	DEVINE	
Devine H.S.		Warhorses
	DEWEYVILLE	
Deweyville H.S.		Pirates

High School	Town	Mascot
	DIANA	
New Diana H.S.		Eagles
	DIBOLL	
Diboll H.S.		Lumber-jacks
	DICKINSON	
Dickinson H.S.		Gators
	DILLEY	
Dilley H.S.		Wolves
	DIMMITT	
Dimmitt H.S.		Bobcats
	DONNA	
Donna H.S.		Redskins
	DRIPPING SPRINGS	
Dripping Springs H.S.		Tigers
	DUBLIN	
Dublin H.S.		Lions
	DUMAS	
Dumas H.S.		Demons
	DUNCANVILLE	
Duncanville H.S.		Panthers
	EAGLE PASS	
E.P.H.S.-Winn Campus		Eagles
Eagle Pass H.S.		Eagles
	EARLY	
Early H.S.		Longhorns
	EARTH	
Springlake-Earth H.S.		Wolverines
	EAST BERNARD	
East Bernard H.S.		Brahmas
	EASTLAND	
Eastland H.S.		Mavericks
	ECTOR	
Ector H.S.		Eagles
	EDCOUCH	
Edcouch-Elsa H.S.		Yellow Jackets

Town High School	Mascot
EDDY	
Bruceville-Eddy H.S.	no mascot
EDEN	
Eden H.S.	no mascot
EDGEWOOD	
Edgewood H.S.	Bulldogs
EDINBURG	
Economedes H.S.	Jaguars
Edinburg H.S.	Bobcats
Edinburg North H.S.	Cougars
EDNA	
Edna H.S.	Cowboys
EL CAMPO	
El Campo H.S.	Ricebirds
EL MATON	
Tidehaven H.S.	Tigers
EL PASO	
Americas H.S.	Trailblazers
Andress H.S.	Eagles
Austin H.S.	Panthers
Bel Air H.S.	Highlanders
Bowie H.S.	Bears
Burges H.S.	Mustangs
Cathedral H.S.	Fighting Irish
Chapin H.S.	Huskies
Clint H.S.	Lions
Coronado H.S.	Thunderbirds
Del Valle H.S.	Conquistadores
Eastwood H.S.	Troopers
El Dorado H.S.	Aztecs
El Paso H.S.	Tigers
Father Yermo H.S.	no mascot
Franklin H.S.	Cougars
Horizon H.S.	Scorpions
Irvin H.S.	Rockets
J.M. Hanks H.S.	Knights
Jefferson H.S.	Foxes
Loretto H.S.	Angels
Montwood H.S.	Rams
Mountain View H.S.	Lobos
NE H.S.	no mascot
NW H.S.	no mascot
Parkland H.S.	Matadors
Riverside H.S.	Rangers
Socorro H.S.	Bulldogs
Sunset H.S.	no mascot

Town High School	Mascot
EL PASO (Cont'd)	
Ysleta H.S.	Indians
ELDORADO	
Eldorado H.S.	Eagles
ELECTRA	
Electra H.S.	Tigers
ELGIN	
Elgin H.S.	Wildcats
ELKHART	
Elkhart H.S.	Elks
Slocum H.S.	Mustangs
ELYSIAN FIELDS	
Elysian Fields H.S.	Yellow Jackets
EMORY	
Rains H.S.	Wildcats
ENNIS	
Ennis H.S.	Lions
EULESS	
Trinity H.S.	Trojans
EUSTACE	
Eustace H.S.	Bulldogs
EVADALE	
Evadale H.S.	Rebels
EVANT	
Evant H.S.	Elks
EVERMAN	
Everman H.S.	Bulldogs
FABENS	
Fabens H.S.	Wildcats
FAIRFIELD	
Fairfield H.S.	Eagles
FALFURRIAS	
Falfurrias H.S.	Jerseys
FALLS CITY	
Falls City H.S.	Beavers

High School	Town	Mascot
	FARMERSVILLE	
Farmersville H.S.		Fighting Farmers
	FARWELL	
Farwell H.S.		Steers
	FERRIS	
Ferris H.S.		Yellow Jackets
	FLORENCE	
Florence H.S.		Buffaloes
	FLORESVILLE	
Floresville H.S.		Tigers
	FLOWER MOUND	
Flower Mound H.S.		Jaguars
Marcus H.S.		Marauders
	FLOYDADA	
Floydada H.S.		Whirlwinds
	FORNEY	
Forney H.S.		Jackrabbits
	FORT HANCOCK	
Fort Hancock H.S.		Mustangs
	FORT WORTH	
Arlington Heights H.S.		Yellow Jackets
Boswell H.S.		Pioneers
Carter-Riverside H.S.		Eagles
Castleberry H.S.		Lions
Central H.S.		Lightning Bolts
Diamond Hill-Jarvis H.S.		Eagles
Dunbar H.S.		Fighting Wildcats
Eastern Hills H.S.		Highlanders
Masonic Home H.S.		Mighty Mites
North Crowley H.S.		Panthers
North Side H.S.		Steers
O.D. Wyatt H.S.		Chaparrals
Paschal H.S.		Panthers
Reach H.S.		Eagles
South Hills H.S.		Scorpions
Southwest H.S.		Raiders
Trimble Technical H.S.		Bulldogs
Western Hills H.S.		Cougars
	FRANKLIN	
Franklin H.S.		Lions

High School	Town	Mascot
	FRANKSTON	
Frankston H.S.		Indians
	FREDERICKSBURG	
Fredericksburg H.S.		Battling Billies
	FREEPORT	
Brazosport H.S.		Exporters
Brazoswood H.S.		Buccaneers
	FREER	
Freer H.S.		Buckaroos
	FRIENDSWOOD	
Clear Brook H.S.		Wolverines
Friendswood H.S.		Mustangs
	FRIONA	
Friona H.S.		Chieftains
	FRISCO	
Centennial H.S.		Tigers
Frisco H.S.		Raccoons
	FRITCH	
Sanford-Fritch H.S.		Eagles
	FROST	
Frost H.S.		Bears
	FRUITVALE	
Fruitvale H.S.		Bobcats
	FORT DAVIS	
Fort Davis H.S.		Indians
	FORT STOCKTON	
Fort Stockton H.S.		Panthers
	GAINESVILLE	
Callisburg H.S.		Wildcats
Gainesville H.S.		Leopards
	GALENA PARK	
Galena Park H.S.		Yellow Jackets
	GALVESTON	
Ball H.S.		Tornados
O'Connell H.S.		Buccaneers

Town / High School	Mascot
GANADO	
Ganado H.S.	Indians
GARDEN CITY	
Glasscock County H.S.	Bearkat
GARLAND	
Garland H.S.	Owls
Lakeview Centennial H.S.	Patriots
Naaman Forest H.S.	Rangers
North Garland H.S.	Raiders
South Garland H.S.	Colonels
GARRISON	
Garrison H.S.	Bulldogs
GATESVILLE	
Gatesville H.S.	Hornets
GEORGE WEST	
George West H.S.	Longhorns
GEORGETOWN	
Chip Richarte H.S.	no mascot
Georgetown H.S.	Eagles
GERONIMO	
Navarro H.S.	Panthers
GIDDINGS	
Giddings H.S.	Buffaloes
GILMER	
Gilmer H.S.	Buckeyes
GLADEWATER	
Gladewater H.S.	Bears
Sabine H.S.	Cardinals
Union Grove H.S.	Lions
GLEN ROSE	
Glen Rose H.S.	Tigers
GODLEY	
Godley H.S.	Wildcats
GOLDTHWAITE	
Goldthwaite H.S.	Eagles
GOLIAD	
Goliad H.S.	Tigers
GONZALES	
Gonzales H.S.	Apaches
GOODRICH	
Goodrich H.S.	Hornets
GORMAN	
Gorman H.S.	Panthers
GRAFORD	
Graford H.S.	Jackrabbits
GRAHAM	
Graham H.S.	Steers
GRANBURY	
Granbury H.S.	Pirates
GRAND PRAIRIE	
Grand Prairie H.S.	Gophers
South Grand Prairie H.S.	Warriors
GRAND SALINE	
Grand Saline H.S.	Indians
GRANDVIEW	
Grandview H.S.	Zebras
GRAPELAND	
Grapeland H.S.	Sandies
GRAPEVINE	
Carroll H.S.	Dragons
Grapevine H.S.	Mustangs
GREENVILLE	
Greenville H.S.	Lions
GROESBECK	
Groesbeck H.S.	Goats
GROVETON	
Centerville H.S.	Bulldogs
Groveton H.S.	Indians
GRUVER	
Gruver H.S.	Grey-hounds
GUNTER	
Gunter H.S.	Tigers
HALE CENTER	
Hale Center H.S.	Owls

Town High School	Mascot
HALLETTSVILLE	
Hallettsville H.S.	Brahmas
Sacred Heart H.S.	Indians
HALLSVILLE	
Hallsville H.S.	Bobcats
HALTOM CITY	
Haltom H.S.	Buffaloes
HAMILTON	
Hamilton H.S.	Bulldogs
HAMLIN	
Hamlin H.S.	Pied Pipers
HAMSHIRE	
Hamshire-Fannett H.S.	Longhorns
HAPPY	
Happy H.S.	Cowboys
HARDIN	
Hardin H.S.	Hornets
HARKER HEIGHTS	
Harker Heights H.S.	Knights
HARLETON	
Harleton H.S.	Wildcats
HARLINGEN	
Harlingen H.S.	Cardinals
South Harlingen H.S.	Hawks
Valley H.S.	No mascot
HARPER	
Harper H.S.	Longhorns
HART	
Hart Jr/Sr H.S.	Longhorns
HASKELL	
Haskell H.S.	Indians
HAWKINS	
Hawkins H.S.	Hawks
HAWLEY	
Hawley H.S.	Bearcats
HEARNE	
Hearne H.S.	Eagles

Town High School	Mascot
HEATH	
Rockwall-Heath H.S.	no mascot
HEBBRONVILLE	
Hebbronville H.S.	Longhorns
HELOTES	
Sandra Day O'Connor H.S.	Panthers
HEMPHILL	
Hemphill H.S.	Hornets
HEMPSTEAD	
Hempstead H.S.	Bobcats
HENDERSON	
Henderson H.S.	Lions
HENRIETTA	
Henrietta H.S.	Bearcats
HEREFORD	
Hereford H.S.	Herd
HICO	
Hico H.S.	Tigers
HIDALGO	
Hidalgo H.S.	Pirates
HIGH ISLAND	
High Island H.S.	Cardinals
HILLSBORO	
Hillsboro H.S.	Eagles
HITCHCOCK	
Hitchcock H.S.	Bulldogs
HOLLAND	
Holland H.S.	Hornets
HOLLIDAY	
Holliday H.S.	Eagles
HONDO	
Hondo H.S.	Owls
HONEY GROVE	
Honey Grove H.S.	Warriors
HOOKS	
Hooks H.S.	Hornets

Town / High School	Mascot
HOUSTON	
Aldine H.S.	Mustangs
Andy Dekaney H.S.	no mascot
Austin H.S.	Mustangs
Barbara Jordan H.S.	Jaguars
C.E. King H.S.	Panthers
Carnegie Vanguard H.S.	Rhinos
Carver H.S.	Panthers
Chavez H.S.	Lobos
Clear Lake H.S.	Falcons
Contemporary Lrn Ctr. H.S.	White Tigers
Cypress Creek H.S.	Cougars
Cypress Falls H.S.	Eagles
Cypress Ridge H.S.	Rams
Davis H.S.	Panthers
Debakey H.S.	no mascot
Dobie H.S.	Longhorns
Eisenhower H.S.	Eagles
Elsik H.S.	Mighty Rams
Forest Brook H.S.	Jaguars
Furr H.S.	Brahmans
Gulf Coast H.S.	no mascot
Hall H.S.	Knights
Hastings H.S.	Fighting Bears
Jersey Village H.S.	Falcons
Jones H.S.	Falcons
Kashmere H.S.	Rams
Kerr H.S.	Tigers
Klein Forest H.S.	Eagles
Lamar H.S.	Redskins
Langham Creek H.S.	Lobos
Lee H.S.	Generals
MacArthur H.S.	Generals
Madison H.S.	Marlins
Mayde Creek H.S.	Rams
Memorial H.S.	Mustangs
Milby H.S.	Buffaloes
Nimitz H.S.	Cougars
North Shore H.S.	Mustangs
Northbrook H.S.	Raiders
Northland Christian School	Cougars
Reagan H.S.	Bulldogs
Sam Houston H.S.	Tigers
Scarborough H.S.	Spartans
Sharpstown H.S.	Apollos
Smiley H.S.	Mustangs
Southwest H.S.	Eagles
Spring Woods H.S.	Tigers
Sterling H.S.	Raiders
Stratford H.S.	Spartans
Taylor H.S.	Lions
Waltrip H.S.	Rams
Washington H.S.	Eagles
HOUSTON (Cont'd)	
Westbury H.S.	Rebels
Westfield H.S.	Mustangs
Westside H.S.	Wolves
Wheatley H.S.	Wildcats
Windfern H.S.	no mascot
Worthing H.S.	Colts
Yates H.S.	Lions
HOWE	
Howe H.S.	Bulldogs
HUBBARD	
Hubbard H.S.	no mascot
HUFFMAN	
Hargrave H.S.	Falcons
HUGHES SPRINGS	
Hughes Springs H.S.	Mustangs
HUMBLE	
Humble H.S.	Wildcats
HUNTINGTON	
Huntington H.S.	Red Devils
HUNTSVILLE	
Huntsville H.S.	Hornets
HURST	
Bell H.S.	Blue Raiders
HUTTO	
Hutto H.S.	Hippos
IDALOU	
Idalou H.S.	Wildcats
INGLESIDE	
Ingleside H.S.	Mustangs
INGRAM	
Ingram-Tom Moore H.S.	Warriors
IOLA	
Iola H.S.	Bulldogs
IOWA PARK	
Iowa Park H.S.	Hawks

High School	Town	Mascot
	IRAAN	
Iraan H.S.		Braves
	IRVING	
Irving H.S.		Tigers
MacArthur H.S.		Cardinals
Nimitz H.S.		Vikings
	ITALY	
Italy H.S.		Gladiators
	ITASCA	
Itasca H.S.		Wampus Cats
	IVANHOE	
Rayburn H.S.		Rebels
	JACKSBORO	
Jacksboro H.S.		Tigers
	JACKSONVILLE	
Jacksonville H.S.		Indians
	JARRELL	
Jarrell H.S.		Cougars
	JASPER	
Jasper H.S.		Bulldogs
	JEFFERSON	
Jefferson H.S.		Bulldogs
	JEWETT	
Leon H.S.		Cougars
	JOAQUIN	
Joaquin H.S.		Rams
	JOHNSON CITY	
Lyndon B. Johnson H.S.		Eagles
	JOSHUA	
Joshua H.S.		Owls
	JOURDANTON	
Jourdanton H.S.		Indians
	JUNCTION	
Junction H.S.		Eagles
	JUSTIN	
Northwest H.S.		Texans
	KARNACK	
Karnack H.S.		Indians
	KARNES CITY	
Karnes City H.S.		Badgers
	KATY	
Calvin Nelms H.S.		Eagles
Cinco Ranch H.S.		Cougars
Katy H.S.		Tigers
Morton Ranch H.S.		Mavericks
Taylor H.S.		Mustangs
	KAUFMAN	
Kaufman H.S.		Lions
	KELLER	
Fossil Ridge H.S.		Panthers
Keller H.S.		Indians
	KEMP	
Kemp H.S.		Yellow Jackets
	KENEDY	
Kenedy H.S.		Lions
	KENNARD	
Kennard H.S.		Tigers
	KENNEDALE	
Kennedale H.S.		Wildcats
	KERMIT	
Kermit H.S.		Yellow Jackets
	KERRVILLE	
Tivy H.S.		Antlers
	KILGORE	
Kilgore H.S.		Bulldogs
	KILLEEN	
Ellison H.S.		Eagles
Killeen H.S.		Kangaroos
Shoemaker H.S.		Wolves
	KINGSVILLE	
Academy H.S.		Pride
H.M. King H.S.		Brahmas
	KINGWOOD	
Kingwood H.S.		Mustangs

High School	Town	Mascot
	KIRBYVILLE	
Kirbyville H.S.		Wildcats
	KLEIN	
Klein H.S.		Bearkats
	KNOX CITY	
Knox City H.S.		Greyhounds
	KOUNTZE	
Kountze H.S.		Lions
	KRESS	
Kress H.S.		Kangaroos
	KRUM	
Krum H.S.		Bobcats
	KYLE	
Lehman H.S.		Lobos
	LA FERIA	
La Feria H.S.		Lions
	LA GRANGE	
La Grange H.S.		Leopards
	LA JOYA	
La Joya Senior H.S.		Coyotes
	LA MARQUE	
La Marque H.S.		Cougars
	LA PORTE	
La Porte H.S.		Bulldogs
	LA PRYOR	
La Pryor H.S.		Bulldogs
	LA VERNIA	
La Vernia H.S.		Bears
	LA VILLA	
La Villa H.S.		Cardinals
	LADONIA	
Fannindel H.S.		Falcons
	LAGO VISTA	
Lago Vista H.S.		Vikings

High School	Town	Mascot
	LAKE DALLAS	
Lake Dallas H.S.		Falcons
	LAKE WORTH	
Anne Mansfield Sullivan H.S.		Bullfrogs
Lake Worth H.S.		Bullfrogs
	LAMESA	
Lamesa H.S.		Tornadoes
	LAMPASAS	
Lampasas H.S.		Badgers
	LANCASTER	
Lancaster H.S.		Tigers
	LAREDO	
Alexander Magnet H.S.		Bulldogs
Dr. Leo Cigarroa H.S.		Toros
John B. Alexander H.S.		Bulldogs
Martin H.S.		Tigers
Nixon H.S.		Mustangs
St. Augustine H.S.		Knights
United H.S.		Longhorns
United South H.S.		Panthers
	LARUE	
Lapoynor H.S.		Flyers
	LATEXO	
Latexo H.S.		Tigers
	LEAGUE CITY	
Clear Creek H.S.		Wildcats
Ed White Memorial H.S.		Mustangs
	LEANDER	
Leander H.S.		Lions
	LEGGETT	
Leggett H.S.		Pirates
	LEONARD	
Leonard H.S.		Tigers
	LEVELLAND	
Levelland H.S.		Lobos
	LEWISVILLE	
Lewisville H.S.		Fighting Farmers
Lewisville H.S. North		Fighting Farmers

High School	Town	Mascot
	LEXINGTON	
Lexington H.S.		Eagles
	LIBERTY	
Liberty H.S.		Panthers
	LIBERTY HILL	
Liberty Hill H.S.		Panthers
	LINDALE	
Lindale H.S.		Eagles
	LINDEN	
Linden-Kildare H.S.		Tigers
	LINDSAY	
Lindsay H.S.		Knights
	LITTLE ELM	
Little Elm H.S.		Lobos
	LITTLE RIVER	
Academy H.S.		Bees
	LITTLEFIELD	
Littlefield H.S.		Wildcats
	LIVINGSTON	
Livingston H.S.		Lions
	LLANO	
Llano H.S.		Yellow Jackets
	LOCKHART	
Lockhart H.S.		Lions
	LOCKNEY	
Lockney H.S.		Longhorns
	LONE OAK	
Lone Oak H.S.		Buffaloes
	LONGVIEW	
Longview H.S.		Lobos
Pine Tree H.S.		Pirates
Spring Hill H.S.		Panthers
	LORENA	
Lorena H.S.		Leopards
	LORENZO	
Lorenzo H.S.		Hornets

High School	Town	Mascot
	LOS FRESNOS	
Los Fresnos H.S.		Falcons
	LOUISE	
Louise H.S.		Hornets
	LOVELADY	
Lovelady H.S.		Lions
	LUBBOCK	
Coronado H.S.		Mustangs
Estacado H.S.		Matadors
Lubbock H.S.		Westerners
Lubbock-Cooper H.S.		Pirates
Monterey H.S.		Plainsmen
Roosevelt H.S.		Eagles
Texas Tech H.S.		no mascot
	LUFKIN	
Hudson H.S.		Hornets
Lufkin H.S.		Panthers
	LULING	
Luling H.S.		Eagles
	LUMBERTON	
Lumberton H.S.		Raiders
	LYFORD	
Lyford H.S.		Bulldogs
	LYTLE	
Lytle H.S.		Pirates
	MABANK	
Mabank H.S.		Panthers
	MADISONVILLE	
Madisonville H.S.		Mustangs
	MAGNOLIA	
Magnolia H.S.		Bulldogs
	MALAKOFF	
Cross Roads H.S.		Bobcats
Malakoff H.S.		Tigers
	MANOR	
Manor H.S.		Mustangs
	MANSFIELD	
Mansfield H.S.		Tigers

Town / High School	Mascot
MARBLE FALLS	
Marble Falls H.S.	Mustangs
MARFA	
Marfa Jr./Sr. H.S.	Shorthorns
MARION	
Marion H.S.	Bulldogs
MARLIN	
Marlin H.S.	Bulldogs
MARSHALL	
Marshall H.S.	Mavericks
MART	
Mart H.S.	Panthers
MASON	
Mason H.S.	Punchers
MATHIS	
Mathis H.S.	Pirates
MAY	
May H.S.	Tigers
MAYPEARL	
Maypearl H.S.	Panthers
MCALLEN	
McAllen H.S.	Bulldogs
Memorial H.S.	Mustangs
Rowe H.S.	Warriors
MCCAMEY	
McCamey H.S.	Badgers
MCGREGOR	
McGregor H.S.	Bulldogs
McGregor Prep H.S.	no mascot
MCKINNEY	
High School #3	no mascot
McKinney H.S.	Lions
McKinney North H.S.	Bulldogs
Serenity H.S.	no mascot
MCLEOD	
McLeod H.S.	Longhorns
MEADOW	
Meadow H.S.	Broncos

Town / High School	Mascot
MEDINA	
Medina H.S.	Bobcats
MELISSA	
Melissa H.S.	Cardinals
MEMPHIS	
Memphis H.S.	Cyclones
MENARD	
Menard H.S.	Yellow Jackets
MERCEDES	
Mercedes H.S.	Tigers
MERIDIAN	
Meridian H.S.	Yellow Jackets
MERIT	
Bland H.S.	Tigers
MERKEL	
Merkel H.S.	Badgers
MERTZON	
Irion H.S.	Hornets
MESQUITE	
Horn H.S.	Chargers
Mesquite H.S.	Skeeters
North Mesquite H.S.	Stallions
Poteet H.S.	Pirates
West Mesquite H.S.	Wranglers
MEXIA	
Mexia H.S.	Blackcats
MIDLAND	
Greenwood H.S.	Rangers
Lee H.S.	Rebels
Midland H.S.	Bulldogs
Rowe H.S.	Warriors
MIDLOTHIAN	
Midlothian H.S.	Panthers
MILANO	
Milano H.S.	Eagles
MILES	
Miles H.S.	Bulldogs

High School	Town	Mascot
	MILLSAP	
Millsap H.S.		Bulldogs
	MINEOLA	
Mineola H.S.		Yellow Jackets
	MINERAL WELLS	
Mineral Wells H.S.		Rams
	MISSION	
Mission H.S.		Eagles
Sharyland H.S.		Rattlers
Veterans Memorial H.S.		Patriots
	MONAHANS	
Monahans H.S.		Lobos
	MONT BELVIEU	
Barbers Hill H.S.		Eagles
	MONTGOMERY	
Montgomery H.S.		Bears
	MOODY	
Moody H.S.		Bearcats
	MORTON	
Morton H.S.		Indians
	MOULTON	
Moulton H.S.		Bobkatz
	MOUNT PLEASANT	
Chapel Hill H.S.		Red Devils
Mount Pleasant H.S.		Tigers
	MOUNT VERNON	
Mount Vernon H.S.		Tigers
	MOUNT ENTERPRISE	
Mount Enterprise H.S.		Wildcats
	MUENSTER	
Muenster H.S.		Hornets
	MULESHOE	
Muleshoe H.S.		Mules
	MULLIN	
Mullin H.S.		Bulldogs
	MUMFORD	
Mumford H.S.		Mustangs
	MUNDAY	
Munday H.S.		Moguls
	NACOGDOCHES	
Central Heights H.S.		Blue Devils
Nacogdoches H.S.		Dragons
	NATALIA	
Natalia H.S.		Mustangs
	NAVASOTA	
Navasota H.S.		Rattlers
	NECHES	
Neches H.S.		Tigers
	NEDERLAND	
Nederland H.S.		Bulldogs
	NEEDVILLE	
Needville H.S.		Blue Jays
	NEVADA	
Community H.S.		Fighting Braves
	NEW BOSTON	
New Boston H.S.		Lions
	NEW BRAUNFELS	
Canyon H.S.		Cougars
New Braunfels H.S.		Unicorns
	NEW CANEY	
New Caney H.S.		Eagles
	NEW DEAL	
New Deal H.S.		Lions
	NEW LONDON	
West Rusk H.S.		Raiders
	NEW WAVERLY	
New Waverly H.S.		Bulldogs
	NEWCASTLE	
Newcastle H.S.		Bobcats
	NEWTON	
Newton H.S.		Eagles

Town High School	Mascot
NIXON	
Nixon-Smiley H.S.	Mustangs
NOCONA	
Nocona H.S.	Indians
NORMANGEE	
Normangee H.S.	Panthers
NORTH RICHLAND HILLS	
Birdville H.S.	Hawks
Richland H.S.	Rebels
NORTH ZULCH	
North Zulch H.S.	Bulldogs
ODEM	
Odem H.S.	no mascot
ODESSA	
Odessa H.S.	Broncos
Permian H.S.	Panthers
OLNEY	
Olney H.S.	Cubs
OMAHA	
Pewitt H.S.	Brahmas
ONALASKA	
Onalaska Jr./Sr. H.S.	Wildcats
ORANGE	
Little Cypress Mauriceville H.S.	Bears
West Orange-Stark H.S.	Mustangs
ORANGE GROVE	
Orange Grove H.S.	Bulldogs
ORANGEFIELD	
Orangefield H.S.	Bobcats
ORE CITY	
Ore City H.S.	Rebels
OVERTON	
Overton H.S.	Mustangs
OZONA	
Ozona H.S.	Lions
PALACIOS	
Palacios H.S.	Sharks

Town High School	Mascot
PALESTINE	
Palestine H.S.	Wildcats
Westwood H.S.	Panthers
PALMER	
Palmer H.S.	Bulldogs
PAMPA	
Pampa H.S.	Harvesters
PANHANDLE	
Panhandle H.S.	Panthers
PARADISE	
Paradise H.S.	Panthers
PARIS	
Chisum H.S.	Mustangs
North Lamar H.S.	Panthers
Paris H.S.	Wildcats
PASADENA	
Pasadena H.S.	Eagles
Pasadena Memorial H.S.	Mavericks
Rayburn H.S.	Texans
PATTISON	
Royal H.S.	Falcons
PATTONVILLE	
Prairiland H.S.	Patriots
PEARLAND	
Pearland H.S.	Oilers
PEARSALL	
Pearsall H.S.	Mavericks
PEASTER	
Peaster H.S.	Greyhounds
PECOS	
Pecos H.S.	Eagles
PERRIN	
Perrin H.S.	Pirates
PERRYTON	
Perryton H.S.	Rangers
PETERSBURG	
Petersburg H.S.	Buffaloes

Town		
High School		**Mascot**
	PETROLIA	
Petrolia H.S.		Pirates
	PETTUS	
Pettus H.S.		Eagles
	PFLUGERVILLE	
Hendrickson H.S.		Hawks
Pflugerville H.S.		Panthers
	PHARR	
PSJA North H.S.		Raiders
Valley View H.S.		Tigers
	PILOT POINT	
Pilot Point H.S.		Bearcats
	PINELAND	
West Sabine H.S.		Tigers
	PITTSBURG	
Pittsburg H.S.		Pirates
	PLAINS	
Plains H.S.		Cowboys
	PLAINVIEW	
Plainview H.S.		Bulldogs
	PLANO	
Clark H.S.		Cougars
Jasper H.S.		Jaguars
Plano East H.S.		Panthers
Plano H.S.		Wildcats
Plano West H.S.		Wolves
Shepton H.S.		Stallions
Vines H.S.		Vikings
Williams H.S.		Warriors
	PLEASANTON	
Pleasanton H.S.		Eagles
	POLLOK	
Central H.S.		Bulldogs
	PONDER	
Ponder H.S.		Lions
	POOLVILLE	
Poolville H.S.		Monarchs
	PORT ARANSAS	
Port Aransas H.S.		Marlins

Town		
High School		**Mascot**
	PORT ARTHUR	
Memorial H.S.		Titans
	PORT ISABEL	
Port Isabel H.S.		Tarpons
	PORT LAVACA	
Calhoun H.S.		Fighting Sandcrabs
	PORT NECHES	
Port Neches-Groves H.S.		Indians
	PORTLAND	
Gregory-Portland H.S.		Wildcats
	POST	
Post H.S.		Antelope
	POTEET	
Poteet H.S.		Aggies
	POTH	
Poth H.S.		Pirates
	POTTSBORO	
Pottsboro H.S.		Cardinals
	PREMONT	
Premont H.S.		Cowboys
	PRESIDIO	
Presidio H.S.		Blue Devils
	PRINCETON	
Princeton H.S.		Panthers
	PROGRESO	
Progreso H.S.		Mighty Red Ants
	PROSPER	
Prosper H.S.		Eagles
	QUANAH	
Quanah H.S.		Indians
	QUEEN CITY	
Queen City H.S.		Bulldogs
	QUINLAN	
Boles ISD H.S.		Hornets
W.H. Ford H.S.		Panthers

High School	Town	Mascot
	QUITMAN	
Quitman H.S.		Bulldogs
	RALLS	
Ralls H.S.		Jackrabbits
	RANGER	
Ranger H.S.		Bulldogs
	RANKIN	
Rankin H.S.		Red Devils
	RAYMONDVILLE	
Raymondville H.S.		Bearkats
	RED OAK	
Red Oak H.S.		Hawks
	REDWATER	
Redwater H.S.		Dragons
	REFUGIO	
Refugio H.S.		Bobcats
	RICHARDS	
Richards H.S.		Panthers
	RICHARDSON	
Berkner H.S.		Rams
Pearce H.S.		Mustangs
Richardson H.S.		Eagles
	RICHMOND	
Foster H.S.		Falcons
	RIO GRANDE CITY	
Rio Grande City H.S.		Rattlers
	RIO HONDO	
Rio Hondo H.S.		Bobcats
	RIO VISTA	
Rio Vista H.S.		Eagles
	RISING STAR	
Rising Star H.S.		Wildcats
	RIVIERA	
Kaufer H.S.		Seahawks
	ROBERT LEE	
Robert Lee H.S.		Steers

High School	Town	Mascot
	ROBINSON	
Robinson H.S.		Rockets
	ROBSTOWN	
Robstown H.S.		Cotton Pickers
	ROBY	
Roby H.S.		Lions
	ROCKDALE	
Rockdale H.S.		Tigers
	ROCKPORT	
Rockport-Fulton H.S.		Pirates
	ROCKSPRINGS	
Rocksprings H.S.		Angoras
	ROCKWALL	
Rockwall H.S.		Yellow Jackets
	ROGERS	
Rogers H.S.		Eagles
	ROMA	
Roma H.S.		Gladiators
	ROSEBUD	
Rosebud-Lott H.S.		Cougars
	ROSENBERG	
B.F. Terry H.S.		Rangers
Lamar Consolidated H.S.		Mustangs
	ROTAN	
Rotan H.S.		Yellow Ham-mers
	ROUND ROCK	
New H.S.-Southeast		no mascot
Round Rock H.S.		Dragons
Stony Point H.S.		Tigers
	ROWLETT	
Rowlett H.S.		Eagles
	ROXTON	
Roxton H.S.		Lions

Town High School	Mascot
ROYSE CITY	
Royse City H.S.	Bulldogs
RUNGE	
Runge H.S.	Yellow Jackets
RUSK	
Rusk H.S.	Eagles
SABINAL	
Sabinal H.S.	Yellow Jackets
SACHSE	
Sachse H.S.	Sharks
SADLER	
S And S Consolidated H.S.	Rams
SAINT JO	
Saint Jo H.S.	Flyers
SALADO	
Salado H.S.	Eagles
SAN ANGELO	
Central H.S.	Bobcats
Grape Creek H.S.	Eagles
Lake View H.S.	Chiefs
SAN ANTONIO	
Alamo Heights H.S.	Mules
Brackenridge H.S.	Eagles
Burbank H.S.	Bulldogs
Churchill H.S.	Chargers
East Central H.S.	Hornets
Edison H.S.	Golden Bears
Fox Technical H.S.	Buffaloes
Harlandale H.S.	Indians
Highlands H.S.	Owls
Holmes H.S.	Huskies
Jefferson H.S.	Mustangs
John F. Kennedy H.S.	Rockets
John Jay H.S.	Mustangs
Lanier H.S.	Voks
Lee H.S.	Volunteers
MacArthur H.S.	Brahmas
Madison H.S.	Mavericks
Marshall H.S.	Rams
McCollum H.S.	Cowboys
Memorial H.S.	Minutmen
Reagan H.S.	Rattlers
Robert G. Cole Jr./Sr. H.S.	Cougars
Roosevelt H.S.	Rough Riders
SAN ANTONIO (Cont'd)	
Sam Houston H.S.	Hurricanes
South San Antonio H.S. West	Cougars
South San Antonio H.S.	Bobcats
South Side H.S.	Cardinals
Southwest H.S.	Dragons
Tom Clark H.S.	Cougars
Virginia Allred Stacey Jr./Sr. H.S.	Eagles
Warren H.S.	Warriors
William H. Taft H.S.	Raiders
SAN AUGUSTINE	
San Augustine H.S.	Wolves
SAN BENITO	
San Benito H.S.	Grey-hounds
SAN DIEGO	
San Diego H.S.	Vaqueros
SAN ELIZARIO	
San Elizario H.S.	Eagles
SAN ISIDRO	
San Isidro H.S.	Tigers
SAN JUAN	
PSJA H.S.	Bears
SAN MARCOS	
San Marcos H.S.	Rattlers
SAN PERLITA	
San Perlita H.S.	Trojans
SAN SABA	
San Saba H.S.	Armadillos
SANDERSON	
Sanderson H.S.	Eagles
SANGER	
Sanger H.S.	Indians
SANTA FE	
Santa Fe H.S.	Indians
SANTA MARIA	
Santa Maria H.S.	no mascot
SANTA ROSA	
Santa Rosa H.S.	Warriors

Town / High School	Mascot
SARATOGA	
West Hardin H.S.	Oilers
SAVOY	
Savoy H.S.	Cardinals
SCHERTZ	
Samuel Clemens H.S.	Buffaloes
SCHULENBURG	
Schulenburg H.S.	Shorthorns
SCURRY	
Scurry-Rosser H.S.	Wildcats
SEAGOVILLE	
Seagoville H.S.	Dragons
SEAGRAVES	
Seagraves H.S.	Eagles
SEALY	
Sealy H.S.	Tigers
SEGUIN	
Seguin H.S.	Matadors
SEMINOLE	
Seminole H.S.	Indians
SEYMOUR	
Seymour H.S.	Panthers
SHALLOWATER	
Shallowater H.S.	Mustangs
SHAMROCK	
Shamrock H.S.	Fighting Irish
SHEPHERD	
Shepherd H.S.	Pirates
SHERMAN	
Sherman H.S.	Bearcats
SHINER	
Shiner H.S.	Comanches
SILSBEE	
Silsbee H.S.	Tigers
SIMMS	
James Bowie H.S.	Pirates
SINTON	
Sinton H.S.	Pirates
SKIDMORE	
Skidmore-Tynan H.S.	Bobcats
SLATON	
Slaton H.S.	Tigers
SMITHVILLE	
Smithville H.S.	Tigers
SMYER	
Smyer H.S.	Bobcats
SNYDER	
Snyder H.S.	Tigers
SOUTH HOUSTON	
South Houston H.S.	Trojans
SOMERSET	
Somerset H.S.	Bulldogs
SOMERVILLE	
Somerville H.S.	Yeguas
SONORA	
Sonora H.S.	Broncos
SOUR LAKE	
Hardin-Jefferson H.S.	Hawks
SPEARMAN	
Spearman H.S.	Lynx
SPLENDORA	
Splendora H.S.	Wildcats
SPRING	
Klein Collins H.S.	Tigers
Klein Oak H.S.	Panthers
Spring H.S.	Lions
SPRING BRANCH	
Smithson Valley H.S.	Rangers
SPRINGTOWN	
Springtown H.S.	Porcupines
SPURGER	
Spurger H.S.	Pirates

High School	Town	Mascot
	STAFFORD	
Stafford H.S.		Spartans
	STAMFORD	
Stamford H.S.		Bulldogs
	STANTON	
Stanton H.S.		Buffaloes
	STEPHENVILLE	
Stephenville H.S.		Yellow Jackets
	STERLING CITY	
Sterling City H.S.		Eagles
	STINNETT	
West Texas H.S.		Comanches
	STOCKDALE	
Stockdale H.S.		Brahmas
	STRATFORD	
Stratford H.S.		Elks
	SUDAN	
Sudan H.S.		Hornets
	SUGARLAND	
Clements H.S.		Rangers
Dulles H.S.		Vikings
George Bush H.S.		Broncos
Hightower H.S.		Hurricane
Kempner H.S.		Cougars
Lawrence E. Elkins H.S.		Knights
Stephen F. Austin H.S.		Bulldogs
Thurgood Marshall H.S.		Buffalo
Willowridge H.S.		Eagles
	SULPHUR SPRINGS	
North Hopkins H.S.		Panthers
Sulphur Springs H.S.		Wildcats
	SUNDOWN	
Sundown H.S.		Rough
	SUNRAY	
Sunray H.S.		Bobcats
	SWEENY	
Sweeny H.S.		Bulldogs
	SWEETWATER	
Sweetwater H.S.		Mustangs

High School	Town	Mascot
	TAFT	
Taft H.S.		Grey-hounds
	TAHOKA	
Tahoka H.S.		Bulldogs
	TATUM	
Tatum H.S.		Eagles
	TAYLOR	
Taylor H.S.		Ducks
	TEAGUE	
Teague H.S.		Lions
	TEMPLE	
Temple H.S.		Wildcats
	TENAHA	
Tenaha H.S.		Tigers
	TERLINGUA	
Big Bend H.S.		no mascot
	TERRELL	
Terrell H.S.		no mascot
	TEXARKANA	
Liberty-Eylau H.S.		Leopards
Pleasant Grove H.S.		Hawks
Texas H.S.		Tigers
	TEXAS CITY	
Texas City H.S.		Stingarees
	THE COLONY	
The Colony H.S.		Cougars
	THE WOODLANDS	
The Woodlands H.S.		High-landers
McCullough Campus		High-landers
	THORNDALE	
Thorndale H.S.		Bulldogs
	THRALL	
Thrall H.S.		Tigers
	THREE RIVERS	
Three Rivers H.S.		Bulldogs

High School	Town	Mascot
	THROCKMORTON	
Throckmorton H.S.		Greyhounds
	TIMPSON	
Timpson H.S.		Bears
	TIVOLI	
Austwell-Tivoli H.S.		Redfish
	TOM BEAN	
Tom Bean H.S.		Tomcats
	TOMBALL	
Tomball H.S.		Cougars
	TORNILLO	
Tornillo H.S.		Coyotes
	TRENTON	
Trenton H.S.		Tigers
	TRINITY	
Trinity H.S.		Tigers
	TROUP	
Troup H.S.		Tigers
	TROY	
Troy H.S.		Trojans
	TULIA	
Tulia H.S.		Hornets
	TUSCOLA	
Jim Ned H.S.		Indians
	TYLER	
Chapel Hill H.S.		Bulldogs
John Tyler H.S.		Lions
Robert E. Lee H.S.		Red Raiders
	UNIVERSAL CITY	
Randolph H.S.		RoHawks
	UVALDE	
Uvalde H.S.		Coyotes
	VALLEY MILLS	
Valley Mills H.S.		Eagles
	VALLEY VIEW	
Valley View H.S.		Eagles

High School	Town	Mascot
	VAN	
Van H.S.		Vandals
	VAN ALSTYNE	
Van Alstyne H.S.		Panthers
	VAN HORN	
Van Horn H.S.		Eagles
	VAN VLECK	
Van Vleck H.S.		Leopards
	VANDERBILT	
Industrial H.S.		Cobras
	VEGA	
Vega H.S.		Long-horns
	VENUS	
Venus H.S.		Bulldogs
	VERIBEST	
Veribest H.S.		Falcons
	VERNON	
Vernon H.S.		Lions
	VICTORIA	
Memorial H.S.		Vipers
St. Joseph H.S.		Flyers
	VIDOR	
Vidor H.S.		Pirates
	WACO	
Connally H.S.		Cadets
La Vega H.S.		Pirates
Reicher Catholic H.S.		Cougars
Waco H.S.		Lions
	WALL	
Wall H.S.		Hawks
	WALLER	
Waller H.S.		Bulldogs
	WALLIS	
Brazos H.S.		Cougars
	WARREN	
Warren H.S.		Warriors

High School	Town	Mascot
	WASKOM	
Waskom H.S.		Wildcats
	WATER VALLEY	
Water Valley H.S.		Wildcats
	WAXAHACHIE	
Waxahachie H.S.		Indians
	WEATHERFORD	
Weatherford H.S.		Kangaroos
	WEIMAR	
Weimar H.S.		Wildcats
	WELCH	
Dawson School		Bulldogs
	WELLINGTON	
Wellington H.S.		Skyrockets
	WELLMAN	
Wellman-Union School		Wildcats
	WELLS	
Wells H.S.		Pirates
	WESLACO	
Weslaco East H.S.		Wildcats
Weslaco H.S.		Panthers
	WEST	
West H.S.		Trojans
	WEST COLUMBIA	
Columbia H.S.		Roughnecks
	WHARTON	
Wharton H.S.		Tigers
	WHITE DEER	
White Deer H.S.		Bucks
	WHITE OAK	
White Oak H.S.		Roughnecks
	WHITE SETTLEMENT	
Brewer H.S.		Bears
Meza H.S.		Gryphon
	WHITEFACE	
Whiteface H.S.		Antelope

High School	Town	Mascot
	WHITEHOUSE	
Whitehouse H.S.		Wildcats
	WHITESBORO	
Whitesboro H.S.		Bearcats
	WHITEWRIGHT	
Whitewright H.S.		Tigers
	WHITNEY	
Whitney H.S.		Wildcats
	WICHITA FALLS	
City View		Mustangs
Hirschi H.S.		Huskies
Rider H.S.		Raiders
Wichita Falls H.S.		Coyotes
	WILLIS	
Willis H.S.		Wildkats
	WILLS POINT	
Wills Point H.S.		Tigers
	WIMBERLEY	
Wimberley H.S.		Texans
	WINDTHORST	
Windthorst H.S.		Trojans
	WINK	
Wink H.S.		Wildcats
	WINNIE	
East Chambers H.S.		Buccaneers
	WINNSBORO	
Winnsboro H.S.		Red Raiders
	WINONA	
Winona H.S.		Wildcats
	WINTERS	
Winters H.S.		Blizzards
	WODEN	
Woden H.S.		Eagles
	WOLFE CITY	
Wolfe City H.S.		Wolves
	WOODSBORO	
Woodsboro H.S.		Eagles

High School	Town	Mascot
	WOODSON	
Woodson School		Cowboys
	WOODVILLE	
Woodville H.S.		Eagles
	WORTHAM	
Wortham H.S.		Bulldogs
	WYLIE	
Wylie H.S.		Pirates
	YOAKUM	
Yoakum H.S.		Bulldogs
	YOE	
Yoe H.S.		Yoemen
	YORKTOWN	
Yorktown H.S.		Wildcats
	ZAPATA	
Zapata H.S.		Hawks
	ZEPHYR	
Zephyr H.S.		Bulldogs

Index of Texas High School Mascots

Sorted by Mascot Name

High School	Mascot Town
AGGIES	
Poteet H.S.	Poteet
ANGELS	
Incarnate Word H.S.	Corpus Christi
Loretto H.S.	El Paso
ANGORAS	
Rocksprings H.S.	Rocksprings
ANTELOPE	
Abernathy H.S.	Abernathy
Post H.S.	Post
Whiteface H.S.	Whiteface
ANTLERS	
Tivy H.S.	Kerrville
APACHES	
Gonzalez H.S.	Gonzalez
APOLLOS	
Sharpstown H.S.	Houston
ARMADILLOS	
San Saba H.S.	San Saba
AZTECS	
El Dorado H.S.	El Paso
BADGERS	
Ben Bolt-Pal Blanco H.S.	Ben Bolt
Bishop H.S.	Bishop
Bruni H.S.	Bruni
Karnes City H.S.	Karnes City
Lampasas H.S.	Lampasas
McCamey H.S.	McCamey
Merkel H.S.	Merkel
BATTLING BILLIES	
Fredricksburg H.S.	Fredericksburg
BEARCATS	
Aledo H.S.	Aledo
Ballinger H.S.	Ballinger
Beckville Jr./Sr. H.S.	Beckville
De Leon H.S.	De Leon
Hawley H.S.	Hawley
Henrietta H.S.	Henrietta
Moody H.S.	Moody
Pilot Point H.S.	Pilot Point
Sherman H.S.	Sherman
Whitesboro H.S.	Whitesboro

High School	Mascot Town
BEARKATS	
Glasscock County H.S.	Garden City
Klein H.S.	Klein
Raymondville H.S.	Raymond-ville
BEARS	
Baird H.S.	Baird
Bastrop H.S.	Bastrop
Bowie H.S.	Bowie
Brownsboro H.S.	Brownsboro
West Oso H.S.	Corpus Christi
South Oak Cliff H.S.	Dallas
Dekalb H.S.	Dekalb
Frost H.S.	Frost
Gladewater H.S.	Gladewater
LaVernia H.S.	LaVernia
Montgomery H.S.	Montgom-ery
Little Cypress Mauriceville	Orange
PSJA H.S.	San Juan
Timpson H.S.	Timpson
Brewer H.S.	White Set-tlement
BEAVERS	
Falls City H.S.	Falls City
BEES	
Academy H.S.	Little River
BISON	
Buffalo H.S.	Buffalo
Sunset H.S.	Dallas
BLACKCATS	
Bay City H.S.	Bay City
Mexia H.S.	Mexia
BLIZZARDS	
Winters H.S.	Winters
BLUECATS	
Coleman H.S.	Coleman
BLUE DEVILS	
Celeste H.S.	Celeste
Central Heights H.S.	Nacogdo-ches
Presidio H.S.	Presidio

High School	Town
BLUE JAYS	
Needville H.S.	Needville
BLUE RAIDERS	
Bell H.S.	Hurst
BOBCATS	
Bloomington H.S.	Bloomington
Celina H.S.	Celina
Childress H.S.	Childress
Comfort H.S.	Comfort
Cy-Fair H.S.	Cypress
Dimmitt H.S.	Dimmitt
Edinburg H.S.	Edinburg
Fruitvale H.S.	Fruitvale
Hallsville H.S.	Hallsville
Hempstead H.S.	Hempstead
Krum H.S.	Krum
Cross Roads H.S.	Malakoff
Medina H.S.	Medina
Newcastle H.S.	Newcastle
Orangefield H.S.	Orangefield
Refugio H.S.	Refugio
Rio Hondo H.S.	Rio Hondo
Central H.S.	San Angelo
South San Antonio H.S.	San Antonio
Skidmore-Tynan H.S.	Skidmore
Smyer H.S.	Smyer
Sunray H.S.	Sunray
BOBKATZ	
Moulton H.S.	Moulton
BRAHMANS	
Furr H.S.	Houston
BRAHMAS	
Bellville H.S.	Bellville
East Bernard H.S.	East Bernard
Hallettsville H.S.	Hallettsville
H.M. King H.S.	Kingsville
Pewitt H.S.	Omaha
MacArthur H.S.	San Antonio
Stockdale H.S.	Stockdale
BRAVES	
Iraan H.S.	Iraan
BRONCOS	
Clarendon H.S.	Clarendon
Dayton H.S.	Dayton
Denton H.S.	Denton
Ryan H.S.	Denton
BRONCOS (Cont'd)	
Meadow H.S.	Meadow
Odessa H.S.	Odessa
Sonora H.S.	Sonora
George Bush H.S.	Sugarland
BRUINS	
West Brook Sr. H.S.	Beaumont
BUCCANEERS	
Brazoswood H.S.	Freeport
O'Connell H.S.	Galveston
East Chambers H.S.	Winnie
BUCKAROOS	
Breckenridge H.S.	Breckenridge
Freer H.S.	Freer
BUCKEYES	
Gilmer H.S.	Gilmer
BUCKS	
White Deer H.S.	White Deer
BUFFALOES	
Cross Plains H.S.	Cross Plains
Florence H.S.	Florence
Giddings H.S.	Giddings
Halton H.S.	Haltom City
Milby H.S.	Houston
Lone Oak H.S.	Lone Oak
Petersburg H.S.	Petersburg
Fox Technical H.S.	San Antonio
Samuel Clemens H.S.	Schertz
Stanton H.S.	Stanton
Thurgood Marshall H.S.	Sugarland
BULLDOGS	
Wylie H.S.	Abilene
Alvord H.S.	Alvord
Anton H.S.	Anton
Bowie H.S.	Austin
Avery H.S.	Avery
Avinger H.S.	Avinger
Bandera H.S.	Bandera
Banquete H.S.	Banquete
Bartlett H.S.	Bartlett

High School	Mascot Town
BULLDOGS (Cont'd)	
Monsignor Kelly H.S.	Beaumont
Boling H.S.	Boling
Borger H.S.	Borger
Brady H.S.	Brady
Broaddus H.S.	Broaddus
Burkburnett H.S.	Burkburnett
Burnet H.S.	Burnet
Carthage H.S.	Carthage
Clyde H.S.	Clyde
Coahoma H.S.	Coahoma
Colmesneil H.S.	Colmesneil
Cooper H.S.	Cooper
Copperas Cove H.S.	Copperas Cove
Corrigan-Camden H.S.	Corrigan
Crockett H.S.	Crockett
Dallas H.S.	Dallas
Edgewood H.S.	Edgewood
Socorro H.S.	El Paso
Eustace H.S.	Eustace
Everman H.S.	Everman
Trimble Technical H.S.	Fort Worth
Garrison H.S.	Garrison
Centerville H.S.	Groveton
Hamilton H.S.	Hamilton
Hitchcock H.S.	Hitchcock
Reagan H.S.	Houston
Howe H.S.	Howe
Iola H.S.	Iola
Jasper H.S.	Jasper
Jefferson H.S.	Jefferson
Kilgore H.S.	Kilgore
LaPorte H.S.	LaPorte
LaPryor H.S.	LaPryor
Alexander Magnet H.S.	Laredo
John B Alexander H.S.	Laredo
Lyford H.S.	Lyford
Magnolia H.S.	Magnolia
Marion H.S.	Marion
Marlin H.S.	Marlin
McAllen H.S.	McAllen
McGregor H.S.	McGregor
McKinney North H.S.	McKinney
Midland H.S.	Midland
Miles H.S.	Miles
Millsap H.S.	Millsap
Mullin H.S.	Mullin
Nederland H.S.	Nederland
New Waverly H.S.	New Waverly
North Zulch H.S.	North Zulch
Orange Grove H.S.	Orange Grove
Palmer H.S.	Palmer
Plainview H.S.	Plainview
BULLDOGS (Cont'd)	
Central H.S.	Pollok
Queen City H.S.	Queen City
Quitman H.S.	Quitman
Ranger H.S.	Ranger
Royse City H.S.	Royse City
Burbank H.S.	San Antonio
Somerset H.S.	Somerset
Stamford H.S.	Stamford
Stephen F. Austin H.S.	SugarLand
Sweeny H.S.	Sweeny
Tahoka H.S.	Tahoka
Thorndale H.S.	Thorndale
Three Rivers H.S.	Three Rivers
Chapel Hill H.S.	Tyler
Venus H.S.	Venus
Waller H.S.	Waller
Dawson School	Welch
Wortham H.S.	Wortham
Yoakum H.S.	Yoakum
Zephyr H.S.	Zephyr
BULLFROGS	
Anne M. Sullivan H.S.	Lake Worth
Lake Worth H.S.	Lake Worth
BULLS	
Bridgeport H.S.	Bridgeport
CADETS	
Connally H.S.	Waco
CARDINALS	
Bellaire H.S.	Bellaire
Bridge City H.S.	Bridge City
Columbus H.S.	Columbus
Del Valle H.S.	Del Valle
Sabine H.S.	Gladewater
Harlingen H.S.	Harlingen
High Island H.S.	High Island
MacArthur H.S.	Irving
LaVilla H.S.	LaVilla
Melissa H.S.	Melissa
Pottsboro H.S.	Pottsboro
South Side H.S.	San Antonio
Savoy H.S.	Savoy
CAVALIERS	
Lake Travis H.S.	Austin

High School	Mascot Town
CHAPARRALS	
Aubrey H.S.	Aubrey
Westlake H.S.	Austin
O. D. Wyatt H.S.	Fort Worth
CHARGERS	
Horn H.S.	Mesquite
Churchill H.S.	San Antonio
CHIEFS	
Crosbyton H.S.	Crosbyton
Lake View H.S.	San Angelo
CHIEFTAINS	
Friona H.S.	Friona
COBRAS	
Industrial H.S.	Vanderbilt
COLONELS	
South Garland H.S.	Garland
COLTS	
Arlington H.S.	Arlington
Worthing H.S.	Houston
COMANCHES	
Shiner H.S.	Shiner
West Texas H.S.	Stinnett
CONQUISTADORES	
Del Valle H.S.	El Paso
COTTON PICKERS	
Robstown H.S.	Robstown
COUGARS	
Cooper H.S.	Abilene
Seguin H.S.	Arlington
Crockett H.S.	Austin
Buna H.S.	Buna
China Spring H.S.	China Spring
Crosby H.S.	Crosby
Bryan Adams H.S.	Dallas
Edinburg North H.S.	Edinburg
Franklin H.S.	El Paso
Western Hills H.S.	Fort Worth
Cypress Creek H.S.	Houston
Nimitz H.S.	Houston
Northland Christian School	Houston
Jarrell H.S.	Jarrell
Leon H.S.	Jewett
Cinco Ranch H.S.	Katy

High School	Mascot Town
COUGARS (Cont'd)	
La Marque H.S.	La Marque
Canyon H.S.	New Braunfels
Clark H.S.	Plano
Rosebud-Lott H.S.	Rosebud
Robert G. Cole Jr./Sr. H.S.	San Antonio
South San Antonio H.S. West	San Antonio
Tom Clark H.S.	San Antonio
Kempner H.S.	Sugarland
The Colony H.S.	The Colony
Tomball H.S.	Tomball
Reicher Catholic H.S.	Waco
Brazos H.S.	Wallis
COWBOYS	
Coppell H.S.	Coppell
Cotulla H.S.	Cotulla
David W. Carter H.S.	Dallas
Edna H.S.	Edna
Happy H.S.	Happy
Plains H.S.	Plains
Premont H.S.	Premont
McCollum H.S.	San Antonio
Woodson School	Woodson
COYOTES	
Alice H.S.	Alice
Anna H.S.	Anna
La Joya H.S.	La Joya
Tornillo H.S.	Tornillo
Uvalde H.S.	Uvalde
Wichita Falls H.S.	Wichita Falls
CRANES	
Crane H.S.	Crane
CUBS	
Brenham H.S.	Brenham
Brownfield H.S.	Brownfield
Round Top-Carmine H.S.	Carmine
Clifton H.S.	Clifton
Olney H.S.	Olney

Mascot *High School*	*Town*
CYCLONES	
Memphis H.S.	Memphis
DEER	
Deer Park H.S.	Deer Park
DEMONS	
Dumas H.S.	Dumas
DONS	
Palo Duro H.S.	Amarillo
DRAGONS	
Bangs H.S.	Bangs
Chico H.S.	Chico
Carroll H.S.	Grapevine
Nacogdoches H.S.	Nacogdoches
Redwater H.S.	Redwater
Round Rock H.S.	Round Rock
Southwest H.S.	San Antonio
Seagoville H.S.	Seagoville
DUCKS	
Taylor H.S.	Taylor
EAGLES	
Abilene H.S.	Abilene
Allen H.S.	Allen
Apple Springs H.S.	Apple Springs
Argyle H.S.	Argyle
Akins H.S.	Austin
Harmony H.S.	Big Sandy
Brock H.S.	Brock
Canton H.S.	Canton
Canutillo H.S.	Canutillo
Canyon H.S.	Canyon
Chillicothe H.S.	Chillicothe
Oak Ridge H.S.	Conroe
Mildred H.S.	Corsicana
Crowley H.S.	Crowley
Wilmer-Hutchins H.S.	Dallas
Decatur H.S.	Decatur
De Soto H.S.	De Soto
Detroit H.S.	Detroit
New Diana H.S.	Diana
Eagle Pass H.S.	Eagle Pass
Ector H.S.	Ector
Andress H.S.	El Paso
Eldorado H.S.	Eldorado
Fairfield H.S.	Fairfield
Carter-Riverside H.S.	Fort Worth
Diamond Hill-Jarvis H.S.	Fort Worth
Reach H.S.	Fort Worth

Mascot *High School*	*Town*
EAGLES (cont'd)	
Sanford-Fritch H.S.	Fritch
Georgetown H.S.	George-town
Goldthwaite H.S.	Gold-thwaite
Hearne H.S.	Hearne
Hillsboro H.S.	Hillsboro
Holliday H.S.	Holliday
Cypress Falls H.S.	Houston
Eisenhower H.S.	Houston
Klein Forest H.S.	Houston
Southwest H.S.	Houston
Washington H.S.	Houston
Lyndon B. Johnson H.S.	Johnson City
Junction H.S.	Junction
Calvin Nelms H.S.	Katy
Ellison H.S.	Killeen
Lexington H.S.	Lexington
Lindale H.S.	Lindale
Roosevelt H.S.	Lubbock
Luling H.S.	Luling
Milano H.S.	Milano
Mission H.S.	Mission
Barbers Hill H.S.	Mont Belvieu
New Caney H.S.	New Caney
Newton H.S.	Newton
Pasadena H.S.	Pasadena
Pecos H.S.	Pecos
Pettus H.S.	Pettus
Pleasanton H.S.	Pleasanton
Prosper H.S.	Prosper
Richardson H.S.	Richardson
Rio Vista H.S.	Rio Vista
Rogers H.S.	Rogers
Rowlett H.S.	Rowlett
Rusk H.S.	Rusk
Salado H.S.	Salado
Grape Creek H.S.	San Angelo
Brackenridge H.S.	San Antonio
San Elizario H.S.	San Elizario
Sanderson H.S.	Sanderson
Seagraves H.S.	Seagraves
Sterling City H.S.	Sterling City
Willowridge H.S.	Sugarland
Tatum H.S.	Tatum

High School	Mascot Town
EAGLES (Cont'd)	
V.A. Stacey Jr./Sr. H.S.	San Antonio
Valley Mills H.S.	Valley Mills
Valley View H.S.	Valley View
Van Horn H.S.	Van Horn
Woden H.S.	Woden
Woodsboro H.S.	Woodsboro
Woodville H.S.	Woodville
ELKS	
Burleson H.S.	Burleson
Elkhart H.S.	Elkhart
Evant H.S.	Evant
Stratford H.S.	Stratford
EXPORTERS	
Brazosport H.S.	Freeport
FALCONS	
Bushland H.S.	Bushland
Channelview H.S.	Channelview
A. Maceo Smith H.S.	Dallas
Clear Lake H.S.	Houston
Jersey Village H.S.	Houston
Jones H.S.	Houston
Hargrave H.S.	Huffman
Fannindel H.S.	Ladonia
Lake Dallas H.S.	Lake Dallas
Los Fresnos H.S.	Los Fresnos
Royal H.S.	Pattison
Foster H.S.	Richmond
Veribest H.S.	Veribest
FIGHTING BEARS	
Hastings H.S.	Houston
FIGHTING BRAVES	
Community H.S.	Nevada
FIGHTING BUCKS	
Alpine H.S.	Alpine
FIGHTING COWBOYS	
Porter H.S.	Brownsville
FIGHTING FARMERS	
Lewisville H.S.	Lewisville
Lewisville H.S. North	Lewisville
FIGHTING FARMERS	
Farmersville H.S.	Farmersville
FIGHTING IRISH	
Cathedral H.S.	El Paso
Shamrock H.S.	Shamrock
FIGHTING SANDCRABS	
Calhoun H.S.	Port Lavaca
FIGHTING TEXANS	
Ray H.S.	Corpus Christi
FIGHTING TIGERS	
Bremond H.S.	Bremond
FIGHTING WILDCATS	
Dunbar H.S.	Fort Worth
FLYERS	
Lapoynor H.S.	Larue
Saint Jo H.S.	Saint Jo
St. Joseph H.S.	Victoria
FOXES	
Caddo Mills H.S.	Caddo Mills
Jefferson H.S.	El Paso
GANDERS	
Lee H.S.	Baytown
GATORS	
Dickinson H.S.	Dickinson
GENERALS	
Lee H.S.	Houston
MacArthur H.S.	Houston
GLADIATORS	
Italy H.S.	Italy
Roma H.S.	Roma
GOATS	
Groesbeck H.S.	Groesbeck
GOBBLERS	
Cuero H.S.	Cuero
GOLDEN BEARS	
Edison H.S.	San Antonio

Mascot High School	Town
GOLDEN EAGLES	
Hanna H.S.	Brownsville
GOLDEN SANDSTORM	
Amarillo H.S.	Amarillo
GOLDEN WOLVES	
Dalhart H.S.	Dalhart
GOPHERS	
Grand Prairie H.S.	Grand Prairie
GREYHOUNDS	
Boerne H.S.	Boerne
Gruver H.S.	Gruver
Knox City H.S.	Knox City
Peaster H.S.	Peaster
San Benito H.S.	San Benito
Taft H.S.	Taft
Throckmorton H.S.	Throckmorton
GRIFFINS	
G. Garza Independence H.S.	Austin
GRYPHONS	
Meza H.S.	White Settlement
HARVESTERS	
Pampa H.S.	Pampa
HAWKS	
Hebron H.S.	Carrollton
Harlingen H.S. South	Harlingen
Hawkins H.S.	Hawkins
Iowa Park H.S.	Iowa Park
Birdville H.S.	North Richland Hills
Hendrickson H.S.	Pflugerville
Red Oak H.S.	Red Oak
Hardin-Jefferson H.S.	Sour Lake
Pleasant Grove H.S.	Texarkana
Wall H.S.	Wall
Zapata H.S.	Zapata
HERD	
Hereford H.S.	Hereford
HIGHLANDERS	
Bel Air H.S.	El Paso
Eastern Hills H.S.	Fort Worth
The Woodlands H.S.	The Woodlands
HIPPOS	
Hutto H.S.	Hutto
HORNETS	
Highland Park H.S.	Amarillo
Aspermont H.S.	Aspermont
Athens H.S.	Athens
Azle H.S.	Azle
Caldwell H.S.	Caldwell
Flour Bluff H.S.	Corpus Christi
Gatesville H.S.	Gatesville
Goodrich H.S.	Goodrich
Hardin H.S.	Hardin
Hemphill H.S.	Hemphill
Holland H.S.	Holland
Hooks H.S.	Hooks
Huntsville H.S.	Huntsville
Lorenzo H.S.	Lorenzo
Louise H.S.	Louise
Hudson H.S.	Lufkin
Irion H.S.	Mertzon
Muenster H.S.	Muenster
Boles ISD. H.S.	Quinlan
East Central H.S.	San Antonio
Sudan H.S.	Sudan
Tulia H.S.	Tulia
HURRICANES	
Sam Houston H.S.	San Antonio
Hightower H.S.	Sugarland
HUSKIES	
Chapin H.S.	El Paso
Holmes H.S.	San Antonio
Hirschi H.S.	Wichita Falls
INDIANS	
Alvarado H.S.	Alvarado
Campbell H.S.	Campbell
Cherokee H.S.	Cherokee
Cleveland H.S.	Cleveland
Comanche H.S.	Comanche
Ysleta H.S.	El Paso
Frankston H.S.	Frankston
Fort Davis H.S.	Fort Davis
Ganado H.S.	Ganado
Grand Saline H.S.	Grand Saline

INDIANS (Cont'd)

High School	Town
Groveton H.S.	Groveton
Sacred Heart H.S.	Hallettsville
Haskell H.S.	Haskell
Jacksonville H.S.	Jacksonville
Jourdanton H.S.	Jourdanton
Karnack H.S.	Karnack
Keller H.S.	Keller
Morton H.S.	Morton
Nocona H.S.	Nocona
Port Neches-Groves H.S.	Port Neches
Quanah H.S.	Quanah
Harlandale H.S.	San Antonio
Sanger H.S.	Sanger
Santa Fe H.S.	Santa Fe
Seminole H.S.	Seminole
Jim Ned H.S.	Tuscola
Waxahachie H.S.	Waxahachie

JACKRABBITS

High School	Town
Forney H.S.	Forney
Graford H.S.	Graford
Ralls H.S.	Ralls

JAGUARS

High School	Town
Summit H.S.	Arlington
Johnson H.S.	Austin
Central Senior H.S.	Beaumont
Moises Molina H.S.	Dallas
Economedes H.S.	Edinburg
Flower Mound H.S.	Flower Mound
Barbara Jordan H.S.	Houston
Forest Brook H.S.	Houston
Jasper H.S.	Plano

JAVELINAS

High School	Town
Crystal City H.S.	Crystal City

JERSEYS

High School	Town
Falfurrias H.S.	Falfurrias

KANGAROOS

High School	Town
Killeen H.S.	Killeen
Kress H.S.	Kress
Weatherford H.S.	Weatherford

KNIGHTS

High School	Town
McCallum H.S.	Austin
Justin F. Kimball H.S.	Dallas
J.M. Hanks H.S.	El Paso
Harker Heights H.S.	Harker Heights
Hall H.S.	Houston
St. Augustine H.S.	Laredo

KNIGHTS (Cont'd)

High School	Town
Lindsay H.S.	Lindsay
Lawrence E. Elkins H.S.	Sugarland
W.H. Adamson H.S.	Dallas
Gainesville H.S.	Gainesville
La Grange H.S.	La Grange
Lorena H.S.	Lorena
Liberty-Eylau H.S.	Texarkana
Van Vleck H.S.	Van Vleck

LIGHTNING BOLTS

High School	Town
Central H.S.	Fort Worth

LIONS

High School	Town
Albany Jr./Sr. H.S.	Albany
Blooming Grove H.S.	Blooming Grove
Brownwood H.S.	Brownwood
Turner H.S.	Carrollton
Dublin H.S.	Dublin
Clint H.S.	El Paso
Ennis H.S.	Ennis
Castleberry H.S.	Fort Worth
Franklin H.S.	Franklin
Union Grove H.S.	Gladewater
Greenville H.S.	Greenville
Henderson H.S.	Henderson
Taylor H.S.	Houston
Yates H.S.	Houston
Kaufman H.S.	Kaufman
Kenedy H.S.	Kenedy
Kountze H.S.	Kountze
La Feria H.S.	La Feria
Leander H.S.	Leander
Livingston H.S.	Livingston
Lockhart H.S.	Lockhart
Lovelady H.S.	Lovelady
McKinney H.S.	McKinney
New Boston H.S.	New Boston
New Deal H.S.	New Deal
Ozona H.S.	Ozona
Ponder H.S.	Ponder
Roby H.S.	Roby
Roxton H.S.	Roxton
Spring H.S.	Spring
Teague H.S.	Teague
John Tyler H.S.	Tyler

High Shool	Mascot	Town
	LIONS (Cont'd)	
Vernon H.S.		Vernon
Waco H.S.		Waco
	LOBOS	
Lopez H.S.		Brownsville
Cisco H.S.		Cisco
Mountain View H.S.		El Paso
Chavez H.S.		Houston
Langham Creek H.S.		Houston
Lehman H.S.		Kyle
Levelland H.S.		Levelland
Little Elm H.S.		Little Elm
Longview H.S.		Longview
Monahans H.S.		Monahans
	LONGHORNS	
Agua Dulce H.S.		Agua Dulce
Caprock H.S.		Amarillo
Axtell H.S.		Axtell
Bronte H.S.		Bronte
Cedar Hill H.S.		Cedar Hill
Tarkington H.S.		Cleveland
W.T. White H.S.		Dallas
Early H.S.		Early
George West H.S.		George West
Hamshire-Fannett H.S.		Hamshire
Harper H.S.		Harper
Hart Jr./Sr. H.S.		Hart
Hebbronville H.S.		Hebbronville
J. Frank Dobie H.S.		Houston
United H.S.		Laredo
Lockney H.S.		Lockney
McLeod H.S.		McLeod
Vega H.S.		Vega
	LUMBERJACKS	
Diboll H.S.		Diboll
	LYNX	
Spearman H.S.		Spearman
	MARAUDERS	
Marcus H.S.		Flower Mound
	MARLINS	
Madison H.S.		Houston
Port Aransas H.S.		Port Aransas
	MAROONS	
Austin H.S.		Austin

High School	Mascot	Town
	MATADORS	
Parkland H.S.		El Paso
Estacado H.S.		Lubbock
Seguin H.S.		Seguin
	MAVERICKS	
McNeil H.S.		Austin
Eastland H.S.		Eastland
Morton Ranch H.S.		Katy
Marshall H.S.		Marshall
Pasadena Memorial H.S.		Pasadena
Pearsall H.S.		Pearsall
Madison H.S.		San Antonio
	MIGHTY MITES	
Masonic Home H.S.		Fort Worth
	MIGHTY RAMS	
Elsik H.S.		Houston
	MIGHTY RED ANTS	
Progreso H.S.		Progreso
	MINUTEMEN	
Memorial H.S.		San Antonio
	MOGULS	
Munday H.S.		Munday
	MONARCHS	
Poolville H.S.		Poolville
	MULES	
Muleshoe H.S.		Muleshoe
Alamo Heights H.S.		San Antonio
	MUSTANGS	
Andrews H.S.		Andrews
Martins Mill H.S.		Ben Wheeler
Bovina H.S.		Bovina
Brookesmith H.S.		Brookesmith
Burkeville Jr./Sr. H.S.		Burkeville
Creekview H.S.		Carrollton
King H.S.		Corpus Christi
Roosevelt H.S.		Dallas
Denver City H.S.		Denver City
Burges H.S.		El Paso

Mascot High School	Town
MUSTANGS (Cont'd)	
Slocum H.S.	Elkhart
Fort Hancock H.S.	Fort Hancock
Friendswood H.S.	Friendswood
Grapevine H.S.	Grapevine
Aldine H.S.	Houston
Austin H.S.	Houston
Memorial H.S.	Houston
North Shore H.S.	Houston
Smiley H.S.	Houston
Westfield H.S.	Houston
Hughes Springs H.S.	Hughes Springs
Ingleside H.S.	Ingleside
Taylor H.S.	Katy
Kingwood H.S.	Kingwood
Nixon H.S.	Laredo
Ed White Memorial H.S.	League City
Coronado H.S.	Lubbock
Madisonville H.S.	Madisonville
Manor H.S.	Manor
Marble Falls H.S.	Marble Falls
McAllen Memorial H.S.	McAllen
Mumford H.S.	Mumford
Natalia H.S.	Natalia
Nixon-Smiley H.S.	Nixon
West Orange-Stark H.S.	Orange
Overton H.S.	Overton
Chisum H.S.	Paris
Pearce H.S.	Richardson
Lamar Consolidated H.S.	Rosenberg
Jefferson H.S.	San Antonio
John Jay H.S.	San Antonio
Shallowater H.S.	Shallowater
Sweetwater H.S.	Sweetwater
City View Jr./Sr. H.S.	Wichita Falls
NIGHT HAWKS	
Barbara Manns H.S.	Dallas
OILERS	
Pearland H.S.	Pearland
West Hardin H.S.	Saratoga
OWLS	
Reagan County H.S.	Big Lake
Chireno H.S.	Chireno
Garland H.S.	Garland
Hale Center H.S.	Hale Center
Hondo H.S.	Hondo
Joshua H.S.	Joshua

Mascot High School	Town
OWLS (Cont'd)	
Highlands H.S.	San Antonio
PANTHERS	
Alba-Golden H.S.	Alba
Anahuac H.S.	Anahuac
Aransas Pass H.S.	Aransas Pass
Nueces Canyon J.H/H.S.	Barksdale
Bells H.S.	Bells
Blanco H.S.	Blanco
Bullard H.S.	Bullard
Burton H.S.	Burton
Medina Valley H.S.	Castroville
Colleyville Heritage H.S.	Colleyville
Caney Creek H.S.	Conroe
Cypress Springs H.S.	Cypress
Hillcrest H.S.	Dallas
Danbury H.S.	Danbury
Duncanville H.S.	Duncanville
Austin H.S.	El Paso
North Crowley H.S.	Fort Worth
Paschal H.S.	Fort Worth
Fort Stockton H.S.	Ft. Stockton
Navarro H.S.	Geronimo
Gorman H.S.	Gorman
Sandra Day O'Connor H.S.	Helotes
C.E. King H.S.	Houston
Carver H.S.	Houston
Davis H.S.	Houston
Fossil Ridge H.S.	Keller
United South H.S.	Laredo
Liberty H.S.	Liberty
Liberty Hill H.S.	Liberty Hill
Spring Hill H.S.	Longview
Lufkin H.S.	Lufkin
Mabank H.S.	Mabank
Mart H.S.	Mart
Maypearl H.S.	Maypearl
Midlothian H.S.	Midlothian
Normangee H.S.	Normangee
Permian H.S.	Odessa
Westwood H.S.	Palestine
Panhandle H.S.	Panhandle
Paradise H.S.	Paradise

High School	*Town*
PANTHERS (Cont.)	
North Lamar H.S.	Paris
Pflugerville H.S.	Pflugerville
Plano East H.S.	Plano
Princeton H.S.	Princeton
W.H. Ford H.S.	Quinlan
Richards H.S.	Richards
Seymour H.S.	Seymour
Klein Oak H.S.	Spring
North Hopkins H.S.	Sulphur Springs
Van Alstyne H.S.	Van Alstyne
Weslaco H.S.	Weslaco
PATRIOTS	
Thomas Jefferson H.S.	Dallas
Lakeview Centennial H.S.	Garland
Veterans Memorial H.S.	Mission
Prairiland H.S.	Pattonville
PIED PIPERS	
Hamlin H.S.	Hamlin
PIONEERS	
Boswell H.S.	Fort Worth
PIRATES	
Center Point H.S.	Center Point
Eula H.S.	Clyde
Collinsville H.S.	Collinsville
Crandall H.S.	Crandall
Crawford H.S.	Crawford
Deweyville H.S.	Deweyville
Granbury H.S.	Granbury
Hidalgo H.S.	Hidalgo
Leggett H.S.	Leggett
Pine Tree H.S.	Longview
Lubbock-Cooper H.S.	Lubbock
Lytle H.S.	Lytle
Mathis H.S.	Mathis
Poteet H.S.	Mesquite
Perrin H.S.	Perrin
Petrolia H.S.	Petrolia
Pittsburg H.S.	Pittsburg
Poth H.S.	Poth
Rockport-Fulton H.S.	Rockport
Shepherd H.S.	Shepherd
James Bowie H.S.	Simms
Sinton H.S.	Sinton
Spurger H.S.	Spurger
Vidor H.S.	Vidor
La Vega H.S.	Waco
Wells H.S.	Wells
Wylie H.S.	Wylie

High School	*Town*
PLAINSMEN	
Monterey H.S.	Lubbock
PORCUPINES	
Springtown H.S.	Spring-town
PRIDE	
Academy H.S.	Kingsville
PUNCHERS	
Mason H.S.	Mason
PURPLE WARRIORS	
Bonham H.S.	Bonham
RABBITS	
Atlanta H.S.	Atlanta
RACCOONS	
Frisco H.S.	Frisco
RAIDERS	
Rice H.S.	Altair
Randall H.S.	Amarillo
Reagan H.S.	Austin
Rivera H.S.	Browns-ville
Skyline H.S.	Dallas
Southwest H.S.	Fort Worth
North Garland H.S.	Garland
Northbrook H.S.	Houston
Sterling H.S.	Houston
Lumberton H.S.	Lumberton
West Rusk H.S.	New Lon-don
PSJA North H.S.	Pharr
William H. Taft H.S.	San Anto-nio
Rider H.S.	Wichita Falls
RAMS	
Johnston H.S.	Austin
Del Rio H.S.	Del Rio
Montwood H.S.	El Paso
Cypress Ridge H.S.	Houston
Kashmere H.S.	Houston
Mayde Creek H.S.	Houston
Waltrip H.S.	Houston
Joaquin H.S.	Joaquin
Mineral Wells H.S.	Mineral Wells
Berkner H.S.	Richardson

High School	*Mascot*	*Town*

RAMS (Cont'd)

High School	Town
S And S Consolidated H.S.	Sadler
Marshall H.S.	San Antonio

RANGERS

High School	Town
Sterling H.S.	Baytown
Henry T. Waskow H.S.	Belton
Riverside H.S.	El Paso
Naaman Forest H.S.	Garland
Greenwood H.S.	Midland
Perryton H.S.	Perryton
B.F. Terry H.S.	Rosenberg
Smithson Valley H.S.	Spring Branch
Clements H.S.	Sugarland

RATTLERS

High School	Town
Sharyland H.S.	Mission
Navasota H.S.	Navasota
Rio Grande City H.S.	Rio Grande City
Reagan H.S.	San Antonio
San Marcos H.S.	San Marcos

REBELS

High School	Town
Tascosa H.S.	Amarillo
Travis H.S.	Austin
Rivercrest H.S.	Bogata
Jack C. Hays H.S.	Buda
Evadale H.S.	Evadale
Westbury H.S.	Houston
Rayburn H.S.	Ivanhoe
Lee H.S.	Midland
Richland H.S.	North Richland Hills
Ore City H.S.	Ore City

RED DEVILS

High School	Town
Huntington H.S.	Huntington
Chapel Hill H.S.	Mount Pleasant
Rankin H.S.	Rankin

RED RAIDERS

High School	Town
Robert E. Lee H.S.	Tyler
Winnsboro H.S.	Winnsboro

REDFISH

High School	Town
Austwell-Tivoli H.S.	Tivoli

REDSKINS

High School	Town
Donna H.S.	Donna
Lamar H.S.	Houston

RHINOS

High School	Town
Carnegie Vanguard H.S.	Houston

RICEBIRDS

High School	Town
El Campo H.S.	El Campo

ROCKETS

High School	Town
Judson H.S.	Converse
Irvin H.S.	El Paso
Robinson H.S.	Robinson
John F. Kennedy H.S.	San Antonio

ROHAWKS

High School	Town
Randolph H.S.	Universal City

ROUGH RIDERS

High School	Town
Roosevelt H.S.	San Antonio

ROUGHNECKS

High School	Town
Sundown H.S.	Sundown
Columbia H.S.	West Columbia
White Oak H.S.	White Oak

ROUGHRIDERS

High School	Town
Boys Ranch H.S.	Boys Ranch

SANDIES

High School	Town
Grapeland H.S.	Grapeland

SCORPIONS

High School	Town
Horizon H.S.	El Paso
South Hills H.S.	Fort Worth

SCOTS

High School	Town
Highland Park H.S.	Dallas

SEAHAWKS

High School	Town
Kaufer H.S.	Riviera

SHARKS

High School	Town
Palacios H.S.	Palacios
Sachse H.S.	Sachse

SHORTHORNS

High School	Town
Marfa Jr./Sr. H.S.	Marfa
Schulenburg H.S.	Schulenburg

Mascot High School	Town
SKEETERS	
Mesquite H.S.	Mesquite
SKYROCKETS	
Wellington H.S.	Wellington
SPARTANS	
W.W. Samuell H.S.	Dallas
Scarborough H.S.	Houston
Stratford H.S.	Houston
Stafford H.S.	Stafford
STALLIONS	
North Mesquite H.S.	Mesquite
Shepton H.S.	Plano
STEERS	
Big Spring H.S.	Big Spring
Farwell H.S.	Farwell
North Side H.S.	Fort Worth
Graham H.S.	Graham
Robert Lee H.S.	Robert Lee
STINGAREES	
Texas City H.S.	Texas City
TARPONS	
Port Isabel H.S.	Port Isabel
TEXANS	
Sam Houston H.S.	Arlington
Northwest H.S.	Justin
Rayburn H.S.	Pasadena
Wimberley H.S.	Wimberley
THUNDERBIRDS	
Coronado H.S.	El Paso
TIGERS	
Anson H.S.	Anson
Arp H.S.	Arp
Belton H.S.	Belton
Blanket H.S.	Blanket
Blue Ridge H.S.	Blue Ridge
Brackett H.S.	Brackettville
Centerville Jr/Sr H.S.	Centerville
Clarksville H.S.	Clarksville
A & M Consolidated H.S.	College Station
Commerce H.S.	Commerce
Conroe H.S.	Conroe
Carroll H.S.	Corpus Christi
Corsicana H.S.	Corsicana
Daingerfield H.S.	Daingerfield

Mascot High School	Town
TIGERS (Cont'd)	
Lincoln H.S.	Dallas
Dripping Springs H.S.	Dripping Springs
Tidehaven H.S.	El Maton
El Paso H.S.	El Paso
Electra H.S.	Electra
Floresville H.S.	Floresville
Centennial H.S.	Frisco
Glen Rose H.S.	Glen Rose
Goliad H.S.	Goliad
Gunter H.S.	Gunter
Hico H.S.	Hico
Kerr H.S.	Houston
Sam Houston H.S.	Houston
Spring Woods H.S.	Houston
Irving H.S.	Irving
Jacksboro H.S.	Jacksboro
Katy H.S.	Katy
Kennard H.S.	Kennard
Lancaster H.S.	Lancaster
Martin H.S.	Laredo
Latexo H.S.	Latexo
Leonard H.S.	Leonard
Linden-Kildare H.S.	Linden
Malakoff H.S.	Malakoff
Mansfield H.S.	Mansfield
May H.S.	May
Mercedes H.S.	Mercedes
Bland H.S.	Merit
Mt. Pleasant H.S.	Mount Pleasant
Mt. Vernon H.S.	Mount Vernon
Neches H.S.	Neches
Valley View H.S.	Pharr
West Sabine H.S.	Pineland
Rockdale H.S.	Rockdale
Stony Point H.S.	Round Rock
San Isidro H.S.	San Isidro
Sealy H.S.	Sealy
Silsbee H.S.	Silsbee
Slaton H.S.	Slaton
Smithville H.S.	Smithville
Snyder H.S.	Snyder
Klein Collins H.S.	Spring
Tenaha H.S.	Tenaha
Texas H.S.	Texarkana
Thrall H.S.	Thrall
Trenton H.S.	Trenton
Trinity H.S.	Trinity
Troup H.S.	Troup
Wharton H.S.	Wharton

High School	Mascot	Town
	TIGERS (Cont'd)	
Whitewright H.S.		Whitewright
Wills Point H.S.		Wills Point
	TIMBER WOLVES	
Cedar Park H.S.		Cedar Park
H. Grady Spruce H.S.		Dallas
	TITANS	
Memorial H.S.		Port Arthur
	TOMCATS	
Tom Bean H.S.		Tom Bean
	TORNADO	
Lamesa H.S.		Lamesa
	TOROS	
Dr. Leo Cigarroa H.S.		Laredo
	TORS	
Ball H.S.		Galveston
	TRAILBLAZERS	
Americas H.S.		El Paso
	TROJANS	
Anderson H.S.		Austin
A.C. Jones H.S.		Beeville
Calvert H.S.		Calvert
Smith H.S.		Carrollton
Charlotte H.S.		Charlotte
Coldspring-Oakhurst H.S.		Coldspring
Moody H.S.		Corpus Christi
Cumby H.S.		Cumby
James Madison H.S.		Dallas
Trinity H.S.		Euless
San Perlita H.S.		San Perlita
South Houston H.S.		South Houston
Troy H.S.		Troy
West H.S.		West
Windthorst H.S.		Windthorst
	TROOPERS	
Eastwood H.S.		El Paso
	UNICORNS	
New Braunfels H.S.		New Braunfels
	VANDALS	
Van H.S.		Van
	VAQUEROS	
San Diego H.S.		San Diego
	VIKINGS	
Lamar H.S.		Arlington
Lanier H.S.		Austin
Pace H.S.		Browns-ville
Bryan H.S.		Bryan
L.G. Pinkston H.S.		Dallas
Nimitz H.S.		Irving
Lago Vista H.S.		Lago Vista
Vines H.S.		Plano
Dulles H.S.		Sugarland
	VIPERS	
Memorial H.S.		Victoria
	VOKS	
Lanier H.S.		San Anto nio
	VOLUNTEERS	
Bowie H.S.		Arlington
Lee H.S.		San Anto-nio
	WAMPUS CATS	
Itasca H.S.		Itasca
	WARHORSES	
Devine H.S.		Devine
	WARRIORS	
Martin H.S.		Arlington
Westwood H.S.		Austin
Tuloso-Midway H.S.		Corpus Christi
S. Grand Prairie H.S.		Grand Prairie
Honey Grove H.S.		Honey Grove
Ingram-Tom Moore H.S.		Ingram
Rowe H.S.		McAllen
Williams H.S.		Plano
Warren H.S.		San Anto-nio
Santa Rosa H.S.		Santa Rosa
Warren H.S.		Warren

Mascot High School	Town
WESTERNERS	
Lubbock H.S.	Lubbock
WHIRLWINDS	
Floydada H.S.	Floydada
WHITE TIGERS	
Contemporary Lrn Ctr H.S.	Houston
WILDCATS	
River Road H.S.	Amarillo
Angleton H.S.	Angleton
Anthony H.S.	Anthony
Archer City H.S.	Archer City
Big Sandy H.S.	Big Sandy
Bloomburg H.S.	Bloomburg
Brookeland H.S.	Brookeland
Canadian H.S.	Canadian
Carrizo Springs H.S.	Carrizo Springs
Cayuga H.S.	Cayuga
Calallen H.S.	Corpus Christi
Crowell H.S.	Crowell
Lake Highlands H.S.	Dallas
Woodrow Wilson H.S.	Dallas
Elgin H.S.	Elgin
Rains H.S.	Emory
Fabens H.S.	Fabens
Callisburg H.S.	Gainesville
Godley H.S.	Godley
Harleton H.S.	Harleton
Wheatley H.S.	Houston
Humble H.S.	Humble
Idalou H.S.	Idalou
Kennedale H.S.	Kennedale
Kirbyville H.S.	Kirbyville
Clear Creek H.S.	League City
Littlefield H.S.	Littlefield
Mt. Enterprise H.S.	Mt. Enterprise
Onalaska Jr/Sr H.S.	Onalaska
Palestine H.S.	Palestine
Paris H.S.	Paris
Plano H.S.	Plano
Gregory-Portland H.S.	Portland
Rising Star H.S.	Rising Star
Scurry-Rosser H.S.	Scurry
Splendora H.S.	Splendora
Sulphur Springs H.S.	Sulphur Springs
Temple H.S.	Temple
Waskom H.S.	Waskom
Water Valley H.S.	Water Valley
Weimar H.S.	Weimar

Mascot High School	Town
WILDCATS(Cont'd)	
Wellman-Union School	Wellman
Weslaco East H.S.	Weslaco
Whitehouse H.S.	White-house
Whitney H.S.	Whitney
Wink H.S.	Wink
Winona H.S.	Winona
Yorktown H.S.	Yorktown
WILDKATS	
Willis H.S.	Willis
WOLVERINES	
PSJA Memorial H.S.	Alamo
Springlake-Earth H.S.	Earth
Clear Brook H.S.	Friends-wood
WOLVES	
Mansfield Timberview H.S.	Arlington
Colorado H.S.	Colorado City
Dilley H.S.	Dilley
Westside H.S.	Houston
Shoemaker H.S.	Killeen
Plano West H.S.	Plano
San Augustine H.S.	San Agus-tine
Wolfe City H.S.	Wolfe City
WRANGLERS	
West Mesquite H.S.	Mesquite
YEGUAS	
Somerville H.S.	Somerville
YELLOW HAMMERS	
Rotan H.S.	Rotan
YELLOW JACKETS	
Alto H.S.	Alto
Alvin H.S.	Alvin
Boyd H.S.	Boyd
Cleburne H.S.	Cleburne
Denison H.S.	Denison
Edcouch-Elsa H.S.	Edcouch
Elysian Fields H.S.	Elysian Fields
Ferris H.S.	Ferris
Arlington Heights H.S.	Fort Worth
Galena Park H.S.	Galena Park

High School	*Mascot*	*Town*
	YELLOW JACKETS (Cont'd)	
Kemp H.S.		Kemp
Kermit H.S.		Kermit
Llano H.S.		Llano
Menard H.S.		Menard
Meridian H.S.		Meridian
Mineola H.S.		Mineola
Rockwall H.S.		Rockwall
Runge H.S.		Runge
Sabinal H.S.		Sabinal
Stephenville H.S.		Stephenville
	YOEMEN	
Yoe H.S.		Cameron
	ZEBRAS	
Grandview H.S.		Grandview